REKINDLING THE SPIRIT IN WORK

REKINDLING THE SPIRIT IN WORK

HOW TO BE YOUR SELF ON THE JOB

HOWARD SCHECHTER

STATION HILL OPENINGS
BARRYTOWN LTD.

To Harry Sloan

Published by Barrytown, Ltd., Barrytown, New York, 12507.

Distributed by Consortium Book Sales & Distribution, Inc., 1045 Westgate Drive, Saint Paul MN 55114-1065

Cover design by Susan Quasha.
Text design by Susan Quasha, with assistance from Vicki Hickman.

ACKNOWLEDGMENTS

Thank you, Barbara Lee, for all the ways you helped me write this book.
Thanks, Woody Swartz, for the Mac in Maui.
My appreciation to family, friends, students, workmates, and clients.

Library of Congress Cataloging-in-Publication Data

Schechter, Howard
      Rekindling the spirit in work / Howard Schechter.
         p.   cm.
      ISBN 1-886449-06-6
      1. Work. 2. Work—Psychological aspects. 3. Work—Religious aspects. 4. Self-actualization (Psychology)   I. Title.
  BJ1498.S325 1995
  174—dc20   95-12501
                                  CIP

Manufactured in the United States of America

CONTENTS

INTRODUCTION

Work and love — these are basics.
Without them there is neurosis.

THEODOR REIK

The purpose of this book is to light the fire of spirit in work. When we discover our true Self, our Essence, we can identify with who we really are. Work then becomes the natural expression of our Essence and a joyful experience.

Many of us have never known what it means to work with spirit. We commonly believe that work is an unrewarding obligation that we must accept in order to earn our living. Many of us rail against work, without any hope that there is a meaningful alternative. Whether we are rich, poor, or in-between, most of us find work a part of our daily experience that is cut off from the main flow of our lives.

There was a time when work and life were integrated. Early peoples hunted, gathered, cooked, and defined themselves. It was, in this way, all Life, not work separated from leisure; work and play blended into a harmonious unity. With industrialization, work became rigidly defined. It meant repetitive tasks, done within a strict time frame, and separated from the rest of life. The most common feeling toward work today is that it is an odious obligation that we must perform in order to enjoy the time spent not working.

This profound alienation is becoming unacceptable to more and more people. We are fed up with work as prison. And, in a world dominated by superficiality, work is increasingly seen as a place where it may be possible to find deeper meaning and self-expression.

Meaning can be found in work. The reason it is most often absent is the lack of "spirit" in work.

Spirit is not religion or the institutionalized dogma of any church or sect. In fact, it is the very opposite of institutionalization or dogma. Spirit is aliveness. It is the breath of the Divine, the dynamic energy of God flowing through us. Spirit is the manifestation, in the material world, of the original Source that creates and sustains the universe — it is the voice of the Great Mystery. Spirit is the fundamental element upon which everything is formed.

One need not be "spiritual" to recognize and honor spirit. We have all felt spirit move in us: the sense of awe in the presence of birth; the feeling when we see an eagle fly or clouds floating across a light blue sky; the sense of greatness and power after coming through a dangerous experience; the sensation of having achieved something great, or a simple act of kindness, or a sense of expansion when working smoothly on a team with others to achieve something important.

Spirit is the energy fundamental to the movement of everything. It is the animating or activating principle in life. When we are in touch with spirit, we feel alive. We often use the term "Enthusiasm," (from the Greek *En Theos,* or "filled with God,") to describe contact with Spirit.

If we split spirit out of our lives or deny it in our work, we feel a sense of deadness. The purpose of this book is to bring aliveness back to work, to lead us to an integration of spirit in work.

Integration means bringing all parts of ourselves to work. The element most often absent in our work lives, after spirit, is emotion. We have been trained to believe that emotions are inappropriate in the work place. They are "unprofessional."

Leaving spirit and emotions at home, coming to work half ourselves, makes work a dull, unfulfilling experience.

This book endeavors to help you get in touch with your Essence and your unique, personal Gift. Your Gift is the set of skills, attitudes, and behavior, that you bring to this world, which no one else can duplicate. It is the Gift you offer, and have been offering, all your life. You may not be aware of it yet, but you have it.

Also included in this book are a set of practical skills for growing in your work. It includes discussions of how to process your feelings to release constrictions and blocks that stand between you and satisfying work. It discusses the role of truth-telling, and of taking possession of the projections we cast upon others as ways to become more empowered in the work place.

Rekindling the Spirit in Work opens us to new approaches to gaining information about work through coming to understand the meaning of signs and symbols in our daily lives. It also stresses the importance of instituting an integrated daily practice into our lives in order to fully develop ourselves and our ability to work from Essence.

The last chapter helps us understand the complexity of the environments in which we work and the challenges and opportunities they provide for self-healing and full expression.

Finally, a down-to-earth question is, "Is this practical? Will I find satisfaction in my work after reading this book?"

A woman named Carol came to a "Rekindling the Spirit in Work" seminar a few months ago. She was so lost and insecure about what to do with work, that her career counselor attended with her. Near the end of the seminar, when she was doing an exercise with symbols, she burst into tears and shared her sorrow. "I've been out of work for two years, and to top it off, two nights ago my cat ran away."

One week after the seminar, her counselor called me. She said, "Howard, I have a testimonial for you. You know Carol, the woman I came with last week. Well, her cat came back and she's got a job."

So if you have either lost an animal, or need a job, or both, read this book.

I

Fundamental Principles

1 WHO IS WORKING? ESSENCE & PERSONALITY

It is better to do one's own duty, however defective, than to follow the life purpose of another, however well one may perform it. He who does his work as his own nature reveals it, never sins.

BHAGAVAD GITA

This book is about who we are and what we do. It is about our identity and our work.

Below the surface, at our Center, lies Essence. Essence is who we truly are. When we discover our Essence, learn to identify with it, and understand that our life purpose is to express our Essence in the world, then work can be a wonderful and exciting adventure.

What is most important to understand is that we are essentially Spirit. We are all manifestations of the Divine. At Center, our Essence is a microcosm of the Original Source. The Hindus call this Atman, the part of ourselves that is God. This part of ourselves is a reflection of the larger universal God-energy, Brahman. In Western terms, we can understand this through the Judeo-Christian belief that "man was created in the image of God." We are a microcosm of the Divine; God, in human form.

Around our Essence grows personality. Personality is the small self. It is the character structure we develop in order to survive in the world. Personality is a mechanism that develops out of the need to adapt to the demands of the environment, both physical and social — parents, teachers, and peers. Personality is not who we truly are, but it is who we usually take ourselves to be.

Personality is the central organizing principle unifying an array of sub-personalities. These sub-personalities are various aspects, qualities, and functions of our character. For example, there may be a part of us that wants freedom and a part that wants security. A part that wants love and a part that is afraid to love. A part that wants to acquire money and a part that wants simplicity. We are made up of countless parts, many at odds with each other, but together they constitute our personality.

The important question, then, is, "Who is working?" Is it our small self, a constellation of parts? Is it one part at the expense of another? If so, satisfying work is elusive. If we work from our big Self, from Essence, we are working from wholeness and Spirit. When we are working from Essence, there is satisfaction, peace and joy.

When we discover who we truly are, a divine, Essential Self, work becomes a joyful experience. We can discover a deeper Self and choose that as our identity. When we begin this process, many chronic problems drop away. Work becomes less confusing and more rewarding. We integrate who we are with what we do.

The key to satisfying work is addressing the question of "who we are" before the question of "what we do." When we focus on the what question, before the who question, we can lose ourselves in a maze of conflicting thoughts. For every idea we have about what we should do, a contradicting thought tells us it's not possible. This process goes on throughout the day, until we feel trapped. When this confusion dominates, we feel frustrated, disempowered, and angry.

Life Purpose

Focusing on "Who I am" can break the cycle of confusion and doubt. We discover our true identity. As Essence, the question of work is simple and action flows easily. "This is my path. I can feel it is right for me."

Using life purpose as an organizing principle allows us to frame work in a larger context. It lifts us out of the "stuckness" of contradictions inherent within a narrowly construed focus on vocation and jobs. There are approximately twenty-seven thousand jobs defined in the dictionary of occupational titles. To choose between these categories as a way of framing work is immensely frustrating. Life purpose is a more unified, coherent, and inspiring concept.

The key to understanding our life purpose is to understand the "Gift" we have been given, and the "Gift" we have to offer. To discover this Essence Gift, we have our life history as the only necessary source of this information. We can look retrospectively and see what function we have served for others, what gift have we always been giving. What archetypal role have you consistently enacted throughout your life?

We are each born with a unique contribution to make. For most of us, it is a long journey to discern our unique nature. Many of us never do. What is required to discover our gift is patient self-inquiry combined with awareness. We need to cultivate the ability to look objectively and dispassionately at ourselves without allowing judgment and self-criticism to dominate. We need to drop into our deep wisdom through quieting ourselves and diving below the level of chattering thought. From the place of inner wisdom we can see the truth in our life, "what is so." This information is trustworthy guidance for the present.

The following exercise is a focused way to begin the process of discerning our Essential Gift. It will suggest to us important information about our life purpose. In doing the exercise, it is important to go below surface impressions. It is particularly important to look beneath critical or negative interpretations. If you find that your definition is framed in terms of "negative" aspects, look deeper to the positive role underneath. For example, you may find your archetype is "rebel." You can interpret that negatively. Or, you go deeper to a level where you see that the Gift associated with rebel is lover of independence and freedom.

Everyone has a positive, unique gift to bring to the world, and though you may not be aware of it, you have been giving this gift to the world all of your life.

While doing the exercise, keep allowing a deeper, more universal understanding of yourself to emerge. Look beyond what you may define as "negative" to the gift below it.

(This exercise, like many of those which follow, is best done with the assistance of a "guide." If that is not possible, record the message and have your own voice guide you through the process).

Discovering Your Gift

- Close your eyes and relax. Put your attention on your breath. Allow any tension to be released through your exhaling breath. Feel yourself getting fully relaxed from your toes to the head.
- Think of a work group you are in right now.
- See yourself in that group. In your mind's eye, look at the different aspects and situations of your typical work day.
- Now open to what you feel like in that group.
- Get closely in touch with the feeling. Let some words come to you that describe what role you play in this group. Do not focus on the formal job title, go deeper to the function you serve, the archetype you are in the group.
- Now, bring your attention back to the breath, and clear your mind. Notice your breath as it comes in and goes out. Release any tension that may have built up on the exhaling breath.
- Now, think of a time in the more distant past where you were in a group that was important to you. Get a sense of yourself in that group, what you did and how you felt.
- What was your role in that group? What deep function did you serve?
- Again, let your mind clear through putting your attention on the breath.
- Exhale all tension.
- When you feel clear and relaxed, recall the first group you were in. See yourself there in all the various aspects of your life in that group.
- Allow the feeling tone you had at that time to come in.
- What role did you play in that group? What function did you serve in the first group you were in?
- Now what is the common theme that runs throughout these roles. Going deeper to the core, what is your archetype in groups? What is your Gift?

This exercise will bring you insight as to your life purpose. It will help you set the issue of your work into a larger framework and shows the continuity of your Essential Gift within the apparent diversity of your work history.

Discovering Your Essence

The Russian spiritual teacher, G.I. Gurdjieff, said, "Man consists of two parts: Essence and personality. Essence in man is what is his own. Personality in man is what is 'not his own.' 'Not his own' means what has come from outside, what he has learned or reflects, all traces of exterior impressions left in the memory and in the sensations, all words and movements that have been learned, all feelings created by imitation."[1]

The *Psychosynthesis* perspective of the brilliant Italian psychiatrist Roberto Assagioli and the *Diamond* approach of contemporary American psychologist A.H. Almaas also define the person as having two parts: personality and Essence. Essence is at the center. Essence is who we are in the deepest and most eternal Self. The personality is a construct of sub-parts that are mostly defensive adaptations created in the process of becoming a person in the world.

As we lead our lives, growing from childhood into adulthood, we find behaviors that are successful in reducing pain and increasing pleasure. These behaviors form into patterns. The most dominant are defensive patterns, habits of mind developed to protect us. Each pattern of behavior may be seen as a template or sub-personality. These patterns, or sub-personalities, taken together, consistent over time, can be called our personality.

Mostly, we take ourselves to be this personality, identifying with one sub-personality after another. Ultimately, this causes us great confusion and anxiety, wondering who we really are and why there is so much internal conflict.

Alternatively, we can choose to identify with Essence; the central part of us, where contradictions fade and we feel integrated and whole; a person in cooperation with himself. When we are identified with Essence, we are "congruent." That is, who we are and who we think we are, are the same. When we are congruent, there is generally a feeling of harmony, peace, and happiness.

When we achieve this identification with Essence, we naturally express it in our work. "It's no big thing." We make natural, incre-

---

1. P. D. Ouspensky, *In Search of the Miraculous* (New York: Harcourt, Brace and World, 1949), p. 232.

mental choices, which move us inevitably into work that expresses our gift. It is not a question of figuring out what we want to do and how we want to do it. It is a matter of being who we are and taking the natural next step.

The following exercise is a vehicle for getting in touch with our Essence. It is a method for discovering the nature of our Essence and a way to identify with it. It is a method for defining ourselves as Essence, rather than as personality.

EXERCISE

Discovering and Identifying With Your Essence

- Lie down or be seated in a comfortable position. Allow yourself to relax. Exhale any tension with the exhaling breath. Relax your whole body, section by section, from the feet to the head.
- Remember a moment in your life when you felt "perfect." When all felt well. When you were at peace. When you felt safe and strong.
- Now, allow yourself to feel this feeling deeply. Get a full sense of the feeling in your body.
- Where is the strongest physical feeling in your body?
- Put your attention on that part of the body completely. Do any words or images appear? Let them "bubble up," appear across your visual screen, or come as a voice in your ear, in an unforced manner.
- Ask the image, if one appears, or ask the feeling state itself, "Tell me the Essence of this feeling." Allow one or two words to emerge
- Now, relax completely by focusing on your breathing. Relax, allow any tension that may have been built up to be exhaled on the exhaling breath.
- Begin again and speak, to yourself, (silently or out loud), "I am_____ ," (filling in the blank with the words that came to you describing the feeling.) For example, "I am love."
- Then, let the full effect of speaking the words to yourself sink into your body slowly and deeply. Open up to this by allowing yourself to breath deeply as the body takes in the affirmation.
- It is important not to rush. Take plenty of time between steps.
- To deepen the experience and become more fully identified with Essence, the affirmation can be repeated silently to one's self as a

meditation a few times a day for as long as you wish. If you do this, the feeling tone of Essence will be brought forward and made a greater part of your daily life.

The key to this experience is coming in touch with the feeling of Essence. It is important to understand, however, that neither the affirmation nor the feeling tone is Essence itself. The affirmation is a vehicle into Essence. The feeling tone is the feeling state associated with Essence. Essence, itself, is a metaphysical entity, beyond the realm of time and space. Coming into relationship with Essence through the vehicle of a personal affirmation is one way we can come to know who we truly are.

Gregg was a television personality who had given up his profession to study and practice psychology. Though he was clear that he was on the right path, he was not clear how he would use his new training and develop it into his life work. Gregg's affirmation, the one that came to him through this exercise, was "I am Compassion."

Gregg was profoundly moved by the feeling this affirmation generated within. He said, "I'm clear that whatever I do, it has to be a reflection of my Essence, and sharing it with other people." He understood that his life purpose, his gift, was the integration of his television skills and his psychological and spiritual insight.

Another professional, Jackie, a lawyer in public service, thought of herself as being in the wrong job. She felt out of place and experienced frustration and stress at work. Through the affirmation development exercise she came to see herself as, "I am Healing." She was deeply moved by this identification. It "felt right," and she was inspired to proceed in her work with newly found enthusiasm.

Jackie saw she was in the right occupation to express her healing gift. Most of her discontent, she realized, had not been with her work but was the result of a state of disconnection within herself. She had been overly identified with various parts of herself and not sufficiently identified with Essence. After the seminar, she was renewed. She was ready to tackle some of the interpersonal issues she had left unattended and contribute more fully to the health of her work group.

Essence and Our Growing Edge

The quality or aspect of Essence that comes through in the affirmation is usually related to our "growing edge," that part of ourselves that is newly emergent. A new blossom of Essence. Essence has infinite aspects: love, truth, joy, compassion and many other qualities. The aspect that actually comes forth for an individual at a given time and powerfully moves him or her to the feeling state of Essence is that part which is most strongly emerging in the moment.

From a psychosynthesis perspective, all emotional life is symptomatic of spiritual truth emerging. The assumption is that whatever we do, we are moving towards greater Self-realization. Everything in the present, and all the past, is an unfolding to a higher spiritual level.

The implication is that it is important to be aware of our present experience because it is tells us much about the state of our spirit. For instance, the experience of stress and constriction may be the symptoms of freedom trying to emerge. Similarly, anger or sadness may be symptoms of compassion welling forth.

Often the feelings experienced on the surface are the opposite of the aspect of Essence that is actually emerging. This is due to the personality structure defending its dominant role against the emergence of Essence. If Essence does emerge, and we identify with it, then the personality structure must move to a secondary status.

The furthest extension of this perspective can be seen in the concept of Spiritual Emergence developed by Stanislov and Christina Grof. It is the Grofs' view that many psychotic breaks are actually "spiritual emergencies." That is, the power of inner spirit is manifesting strongly and is experienced as disorienting. The symptoms, defined as psychotic, are actually the outer manifestations of the emerging movement to a greater level of spiritual development.

A physician in a Rekindling seminar, Phil, was feeling blocked around issues of security and conformity. He had original and creative ideas, which he wanted to implement in his practice but was afraid of the consequences. He identified his affirmation as "I am Freedom." Freedom was the aspect of Essence that was emerging most strongly in him. Yet, in his life he was experiencing constriction. The sub-personality structure was activated and repressing the emergent aspect of freedom. As he repeated his affirmation in meditation, the truth of his need to express Essence through freedom was clear. The fear began to drop away. The power of certainty was generated by connecting with his Center and this allowed Phil to strengthen and enact his personal sense of freedom.

Another client, who felt himself in a menial job, expressed that his feelings were flat. "I hate to say this out loud, but I really feel like I am dead emotionally." In his work to develop the affirmation the words that came were "I am Aliveness." Aliveness was the quality of Essence that was growing. But, his personality structure was in defense and it created and maintained a feeling of deadness. As he meditated with his affirmation and allowed the experience of it to sink in deeply, aliveness welled. The work he was doing began to seem less an issue than fully accepting his own vitality. The challenge was to continue to open to this realization and to patiently allow information to naturally come to him as guidance for his next steps in work.

Because our growing edge is generally the aspect of Essence that emerges most strongly, the affirmation we use to connect with it may change over time. It is not something that changes quickly, however. It is best to let any change in the affirmation happen slowly, without pushing or extending effort.

The affirmation that first emerged for me was, "I am Unconditional Love." This brought me to Center, as it reflected the quality I was needing most to develop; to love myself and those around me. Soon the affirmation shifted slightly, "I am Love." This occurred because it felt more simple, seemed to be more inclusive, and produced the same feeling tone inside.

Two years later, my inner work began to revolve around issues related to truth. I was experiencing a challenge to open to my inner truth and to deal with the fear that it brought me. Also, I was being challenged to speak my truth to those around me, and to deal with the fear of loss and anger that this evoked. My affirmation evolved to "I am Truth." It naturally shifted in meditation without effort or thought.

Disidentifying with the Sub-personalities

Usually we take ourselves to be the sub-personality we are identified with in the moment. If we are feeling insecure, we take ourselves to be insecure. If we are thinking about work in that state, we tend to see it through a lens of worry.

In another moment we are in the sub-personality that longs to be free. At that time, we take ourselves to be the person who wants freedom. We think of work and what we want out of it from that perspective.

Later, at yet a third moment, we are thoroughly confused. "At first, security was all important. Now freedom is everything. What the hell is going on?"

There is no resolution to this confusion and conflict at the level of sub-personality. The sub-parts are of equal status within the personality structure. One sub-personality is unlikely to assume final dominance over another, without the suppressed part rising to renew the conflict.

Resolution comes from identifying with Essence. From the place of Essence, the conflict between freedom and security is not resolved, it fades away. At Essence, there is a unity that includes both the need for freedom and the need for security. The contradiction is dissolved, and often the resulting action meets the needs of both.

The following exercise is an approach to dealing with our sub-personalities that honors and acknowledges them, without identifying with them. This is a delicate matter. To deny a sub-personality is to deny ourselves. It is self-rejection. To deny the insecure part because we don't like it, or to deny the part that longs for freedom because it is dangerous, is repression. The energy will rise at a later time and "get us." It is healthiest to recognize the existence of all aspects of ourselves, allow all aspects to be there, and choose to identify with Essence.

EXERCISE

Disidentification With the Sub-personalities

- Be seated in a comfortable position. Allow yourself to relax. Bring your attention to the breath. Without any attempt to change it, simply focus on the breath, watching the natural rhythm of its in and out flow. Exhale any tension with the exhaling breath. Relax your whole body, section by section, from the feet to the head.

- Bring in the affirmation you developed in the earlier exercises. Be with it. Repeat it slowly, allowing time in between repetitions for the body to accept the message.

- Notice when there is a block or resistance to easily affirming and accepting the affirmation.

- Focus your attention on that block. Allow the feeling in fully.

- Notice where in your body you feel the block most. Put all your attention on that spot. Amplify it; blow it up, let it become big. Let it become all of who you are.

- Now, with your mind detached as if it were on vacation, let the body place speak to you. Let it "bubble up" a descriptive word as a name for itself.

- Use this word, or words, as a name for the sub-personality you just identified. Now, acknowledge that the part is real, it is there. Allow it, accept it, and be clear that the part is not who you are. It is something you have, not who you are. You may "have fear," but you are "not fear." It is a process of acknowledging that the feeling is valid, and not becoming it. Becoming the sub-part is what causes the pain. We **are** Essence, we only **have** the sub-personality.

- *So, make the following statement, first silently inside, then aloud. I **have** this quality_____(fill in the name that came forth), but I am not this quality_____(again, fill in the name) I am_____ (fill in your affirmation).*

The Importance of Positive Self-Regard: Self-Love

To achieve the formidable task of discovering our Essence, it is important that we cultivate a positive regard for ourselves. We can learn to practice Self-love. Most of us in this culture are addicted to self-criticism, it was given to us as children and often framed positively as the path to excellence.

Though it can produce excellence, self-criticism usually produces the opposite. It turns us against ourselves. We become our own worst critic. We become small. Think of how you feel when someone important to you criticizes you. Now, realize that you youself, the most important person in your life, are self-critical daily. From that feeling state, no wonder it's difficult to move easily and gracefully into the "right work." We are staggering around under the pain of self-hatred.

Self-love and acceptance are important because they are the essential elements in inner peace. Self-criticism produces inner conflict: one part of ourselves judging another. This is inner violence.

Acceptance produces peace, unity, and wholeness. There is no inner division with one part of us beating up another. From a place of inner peace, it is possible to get in touch with and accept our Essence and life purpose. With self-judgement and criticism it is difficult to stay connected to Essence.

It is important, therefore, to cultivate positive self-regard and self-love, and to accept ourselves just as we are. To accept all of our sub-personalities, as well as our Essence. From the state of peace this accepting attitude nourishes, it is easier to identify with Essence.

The implication is that we must accept our negative sides, and not reject the parts of ourselves we do not like, or which we fear. The negative parts can shift only if they are loved, and through love, we are empowered to make change.

An important part of this process, paradoxically, is the willingness to accept our self-rejection. We are in the habit of self-rejection. How are we to break this cycle? With more rejection? If we get so strongly attached to accepting ourselves and we reject the part that is rejecting, where is the improvement?

To break the pattern of self-rejection, we must also love and accept the part of ourselves that is rejecting. This will loosen the grip of the rejecting sub-personality and create the "space" needed to allow a shift over time.

Loving ourselves means remembering to consciously give ourselves love. This is particularly important when we are feeling down or beginning to judge ourselves harshly. The moment we notice we are feeling down, (which is often a result of self-criticism), it is wise to scan inside and feel what part of ourselves is rejecting, and what part is being rejected.

These feelings will identify the relevant sub-personalities involved in the struggle. Now, consciously, summon love to the rejecting *and* the rejected parts. This will open up the inner space for a positive shift to occur.

Loving ourselves means being willing to find and engage in work that nurtures us. It is not self-loving to work at a job that hurts us. To do so is an act of self-rejection. The reasons we give for staying in jobs that hurt are seldom sufficient. Money, security, the kids, the wife, etc. They are all important, yet, they need not be blocks to satisfying work.

If we settle for doing a job that we don't like, we reject part of our self. The way out is to love ourselves until the parts that are causing difficulties disappear. At that point we will have the strength and clarity to move into work in which we can express our life purpose.

Most of us wish for more from work than money. We also want social, emotional, and spiritual satisfaction. We have settled for less, because we were told "that's how it is," or "that's life," or "you don't get what you want." Many of us are taught when we are young that "It's not possible to feel good about work. The best thing to do is to settle for security."

A popular bumper sticker passed me the other day. It said, "The Worst Day Fishing is Better than the Best Day Working." It is a measure of how deeply disturbed our culture is, that work is so degraded in the popular wisdom. Most of us work as much or more than we play. If we accept this view of work and play, we are in for much suffering.

Working From Essence

Working from Essence involves discovering the right work for ourselves through discovering who we are and identifying with the deepest, most central part of ourselves. Each of us is the same in this way, we are a microcosm of the Mystery. Yet, we all also have a unique life purpose, a gift to give the world. Our work can be a conscious expression of this gift.

The key to finding satisfying work is first asking the question, "Who am I?" From that, the answer to, "What shall I do?" will flow more easily. Putting the "who question" before the "what question" releases us from the endless rounds of ideas and counter ideas that leave us confused and frustrated.

Even some of the "New Age" maxims around work, like "follow your bliss," or "do what you love and the money will follow," tend to confuse people. "What is my bliss? What is it that I love?" The cart before the horse; "what" before "who." When we ask the Sage question, "Who am I?" and come to understand that we are Essence, then work flows easily and well.

The graphic below summarizes much of what has been said in this chapter.

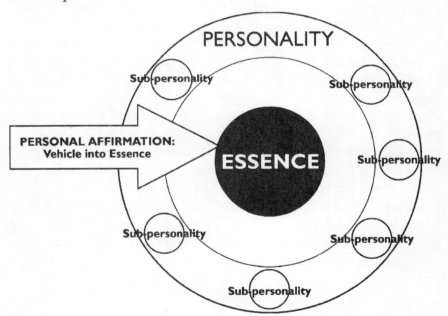

Essence, Personality and the Way-in

2 ☙ INTEGRITY & AUTHENTICITY BEING WHO WE ARE

To thine own Self be true,
And it must follow, as the night the day
Thou canst not then be false to any man
                                                    SHAKESPEARE

Authenticity

Ultimately, what satisfies, is the experience of "being real." Being and acting in a way that is an expression of who we truly are, without posture or facade. When we feel real, we feel substantial and full within.

Despite society's effort to impose conformity and restriction, people who know who they are and express it in their work are admired as people of substance and character. My experience is that people who succeed in the world of work, both independent people and people at the top of organizations, are not conformists. They are people who are fully themselves, and their uniqueness sets them apart.

"Being real" means having integrity. Integrity is wholeness. Nothing essential missing. The integration of all parts of ourselves. Realness involves not rejecting parts of ourselves that are under developed, or which we don't like, or which are "unacceptable."

To be real is an act of courage. It can feel dangerous to be real. Most of us have been hurt many times in our lives, especially in childhood, for being real; for being who we are, instead of the child our parents wanted. This pattern continued with authority figures in school and on the job. For most of us, the threat of punishment for nonconformity has been strong.

As adults, however, it is generally safer to be authentic than to "fake it." Trying to be somebody else is an inherently weak position. We are much more effective and capable when we are our Self. We are generally less capable in the off-balance position of imitation.

Carl Rogers, the founder of client-centered and humanistic psychology, explains what "real" and "authentic" mean. His model is based on the concept of "congruence." To be real, he says, we need to be congruent between three levels. The deepest level, our actual thoughts and feelings, needs to be congruent with the middle level, which is what we understand our thoughts and feelings to be, and with the surface level, which is what we communicate to others about how it is inside.

Congruence, in Rogers' terms, or realness, in our terms, means that each level within us accurately reflects the next. That is, what I am feeling, I know I am feeling, and when I am communicating my feeling, it is accurate and truthful. To develop our realness, then, we have to develop the skills that allow us to have an awareness of what is happening within us, the willingness to face the truth of our inner process, and the courage to communicate it.

Congruence between the first two levels, the inner level of actual feeling and the middle level of accurate understanding of that feeling, is mainly a question of awareness. To know what I actually think and feel takes a commitment to bring my inner process to the light of awareness. Though we often believe our inner life is confusing, it often is not as much confusion as denial; a desire not to accept the truth of a feeling or thought. We don't want to believe we feel a particular feeling because it is unacceptable. It is usually an avoidance based on a moral belief, a "should" or "should not," or a fear.

For example I may begin to feel bored in my work. Immediately I censor the feeling because I will not allow myself to be bored. I have to enjoy my work, so I can be good at it, get a promotion, a raise, and continue to take good care of the family. I will not acknowledge the existence of this feeling because it is "wrong." If I did acknowledge it, I'd be in trouble. My whole world could fall apart.

The truth of the boredom has nothing to do with the consequences of doing something about it. The boredom just is. I am bored and that is that, whether its dangerous, scary, or advantageous. The "wrongness," if there is such a thing at this level, has nothing to do with what I feel. I feel what I feel. More importantly, wrongness, or danger, is not in the feeling or thought, it is in the action that follows.

This is what we so often fail to see. We don't have to deny our feelings or thoughts because of morality or danger. Thoughts and feelings are internal, action is outer behavior. I can lust after my neighbor, the problem is acting on it. And, if I deny that the lust is there, it is likely to emerge in other places that may be even more problematic. It is far better to open to the truth of the original feeling and then choose a course that considers consequences before acting.

I can open to the boredom I feel in my job without quitting. I can open to that boredom, allow it to be there, and acknowledge it. And, I can make choices that are not threatening to my security.

If I deny the feeling because of the fear, then I don't even know what I feel and I am in a position of ignorance and weakness. I can't be real and satisfied in my work because I am not willing to open to what is.

The process follows a pattern. A thought or feeling occurs, we open to it. Another comes up, and because we don't like it, or are afraid of it, we don't acknowledge it. When this happens, we are out of congruence. We are off balance. We are out of touch with how we are. If we act, it will be from a base of disconnection with what is true.

The skill we need to develop is the ability to confront honestly our thoughts and feelings and acknowledge their existence even when we don't like them. It is impossible to be real without acknowledging "what is so."

So, instead of denying I am bored, and having it pollute my work day in ways I don't see or understand, I can acknowledge the boredom and skillfully choose to let it be, without any action. If I wish, I can begin to make a plan to enrich my job or change it.

The second level of congruence involves the willingness to speak the truth of our feelings as best we understand them. This does not imply that we need to "wear our heart on our sleeve," blabbering our insides all the time. It means that when we choose to speak our thoughts and feelings, we speak them as they truly are. Of course, the first level of congruence must be in place for this to happen accurately. We have to know what we actually feel in order to speak truthfully about it.

This is a difficult and challenging area for most of us. It is addressed in greater depth in Chapter Five, *The Power of Truth*. Simply put, we were not, in our formative years, consistently encouraged to speak the truth. In fact, we were often punished for speaking the truth. I certainly was. Many parents supported truth telling when it was convenient. When they wanted to know something from us. Otherwise, the truth, if it was disagreeable or uncomfortable, was seldom welcome.

I remember very well being punished, having my mouth washed out with soap, for speaking my true feelings. "You have quite a mouth on you," my mother would say, or "I don't ever want to hear that again," when she did it.

Teachers and others in authority were often worse. In school, original thought was seldom welcome. I remember my third grade social science teacher lifting me off my feet, from the ear, because I didn't believe what he was saying and wouldn't repeat it aloud in class. Years later, in my adolescence, my high school civics teacher told me that as a potential future leader, I had better begin conforming to acceptable standards of thought and behavior, and let go of my crazy ideas about freedom and independence.

We have a lot to overcome to be real; to speak on the outside what is true on the inside. To heal from our history and to begin to move toward the satisfaction of being real, it is important to remember that we are no longer the child who was abused for speaking the truth. We are adults now, and much of the time we can speak our actual thoughts and feelings without fear. Sometimes, of course, we can't. It may be dangerous, and we need to be quiet. For this, we need to cultivate the wisdom of discretion. Due to our early wounding, however, we tend to overestimate the necessity to suppress the communication of our actual thoughts and feelings, because of remembered, conditioned, and now, imagined, fears about the consequences.

The personal cost for this pattern of a lack of congruence between what we know about ourselves and what we communicate is high. It is the cost of not being real. Not being authentic. In the long run, it gnaws at us. It weakens us, because it doesn't feel right or good inside. It feels safe, but bad.

That bad feeling is not safe. It is the physical manifestation of non- alignment within. It is similar to when our body is out of alignment. If our head is not in line up with our shoulders, and pelvis, and feet, if they are on different planes, our body will suffer. We will be in pain. The strength and comfort in our body, among other things, comes from proper alignment, or congruence, between the body parts.

It important to understand that the issue of congruence between the inner and the outer is not a moral issue, it is a wellness issue. To feel healthy, we need to feel whole and balanced. Authenticity is being real and feeling whole and balanced.

Life/Work Integration

Because authenticity is so central to our well-being, it is important that we be authentic in work. Work needs to be an expression in the outer world of who we are in the inner world. When we do work that is separate from who we are, "just to make a living," we usually suffer. We think we can have a job and have our lives and that they can be separate and that's O.K. In fact, it seldom is, because as we have seen, it's not authentic. It is out of alignment with ourselves and unhealthy.

Life/Work Integration means expressing the truth of who we are in our work. Arnie was an Account Executive with a large corporation in the San Francisco Bay Area. He had grown up on Oahua, in Hawaiian culture, where spirit and daily life are interwoven. As he grew up, went away to college, raised a family, moved to the mainland, and focused on "moving ahead" in his work, the spiritual part of him slipped away. He even gave up a life-long practice of church on Sundays. During a Rekindling seminar, he realized that his work had become unbalanced and sterile. It did not reflect all of who he was. He also realized that he needed to bring the spiritual component back into his life and into his work. Arnie wasn't clear what choices this was going to involve, or what the picture was going to look like, but he was sure that his new direction was right for him. His need to be authentic at work would be fulfilled. It wouldn't manifest in a large outer shift, rather a slight realignment, like a chiropractic adjustment.

Sara was a trainer with the same company. She felt she did not bring all of herself to work. The woman in her was left at home. She had emphasized the masculine to get ahead in the corporate world and "it worked." But it felt empty and incomplete. She began to see that her feminine side, her receptive, supportive, and nurturing qualities were absent at work. During our time together, she realized that if she was to be satisfied in her job, her feminine aspects must be integrated. She was convinced she could be more effective than she was before. Now she would be both strong and nurturing.

The above examples involve people who were incongruent in that they were not expressing an important spiritual component of their lives in their work. Many of us also separate out our emotional life from our work. We try to tear that part of ourselves out and leave it at home. One of the most misused terms I have come across in my work with organizations is "professionalism." What I have most often noticed it to be is a term that rationalizes and elevates the cultural norm of leaving the emotional part of ourself unexpressed in our jobs. "It's not professional." This is one of the major reasons so many of us are off balance at work.

The emotional part of us is seen as feminine and weak. In our macho culture we have decided to keep this "weakness" out of the work place entirely. It is not o.k. to cry at work. Almost all businesses in this country have rigid norms demanding that we leave our emotions and feelings at the gate. We come to our workday only partially ourselves, spending eight hours as partial people. How can that be fulfilling?

This phenomena also has an adverse effect on the productivity of business. Employee creativity, dynamism, and interest suffer. We only get a fraction of the person, only a fraction of potential productivity in exchange for a full day's pay. As long as we demand that our employees leave a part of who they are at home, we will never live up to our economic potential as a society.

A physician at a "Rekindling the Spirit in Work" seminar had a wonderfully uplifting experience as a result of feeling what it might be like to integrate all of himself in his work. Dan was dissatisfied with his job. He was a specialist in eye, ear, nose and throat medicine. He felt his work had gotten overly mechanical and routine.

Through the inner work undertaken at the seminar, he discovered that his profession actually suited him. He touched that part of himself that was a "healer," and as a doctor he had the opportunity to express this gift. He was in the perfect occupation, but because he previously took a limited, unintegrated view of himself, his perspective on his job was too narrow to be satisfying.

Furthermore, he came to be in touch with his frozen feelings; emotions he was unwilling to look at in an authentic way. At the workshop, it became clear to him that he was too distant from his family. A necessary shift, to enjoy his life and work, was to begin to express his emotions and feelings of love and caring to his family and to his patients. As was true with Dan, Life/Work integration often means releasing constricted parts of ourselves and infusing these into our jobs. This actually happens more often than changing jobs or professions.

Conversely, we sometimes make our jobs responsible for what is actually a lack of integration in our lives outside of work. People often blame work for their troubles, because the other major area of their life, relationships, feels too dangerous to probe. It is common for people to wrestle with work issues and find that, in fact, their real dissatisfaction is with their marriage or another intimate relationship.

The corollary of needing to bring all of one's self into work to be real is that if we are not satisfied in our life outside of work, shifting things on the job will not bring us into balance. Life and work simply cannot be seen as separate. They are intimately related, interconnected pieces of a single cloth.

Rhona was a student and a Research Assistant at a major university laboratory. She came to a "Rekindling the Spirit in Work" seminar with the idea that her work was beneath her and she wasn't fully expressing her gifts there. Upon investigation, when she really went within, she found she was satisfied with her work. It was challenging and fun and these were what she most wanted in a job. Rhona didn't mind that she did not have high status or an identifiable career path. She enjoyed her work and that was enough.

At the same time, what Rhona saw was deep distress over an incomplete ending to a relationship that had been over for years. She became aware that she hadn't fully grieved the loss and came in touch with how strongly she craved a new relationship. Though this was a difficult and challenging realization, Rhona felt much better after she understood it. She was in touch with the truth of her situation and empowered to have an effect on it.

What I have seen in my work with people is that we come strongest into our power when we integrate who we are with what we do. As a teacher I have consistently seen graduate students take off on their career path when they integrate the new skills learned with who they were before. Often students think, "I'll learn this field and be one." That is, "I'll study law and be a lawyer." But there is no standard brand lawyer mold to jump into. We all have to shape and create the specific and unique way we are going to do the work we have been trained to do.

The integration of all of who we are with all of what we do is what I call the "power point." The point of integration between one's new skills and old skills, one's attitudes, beliefs, training, and experience. We are at our power point when we are in work and expressing our unique gifts.

Two students who were studying Organizational Development were floundering in a sea of confusion about how to do this work. Then, through some applied projects they came to see how they could integrate their organizational skills with an earlier and deeper interest, Education. Now they have a energetic and growing practice of organizational consulting to educational institutions.

Similarly, a professor on our faculty struggled for years trying to develop his consulting practice until he began to integrate his life passion, Aikido, into his work. He began to specialize in the area of conflict resolution, using the metaphor of Aikido. He began to use the physical moves involved in Aikido to demonstrate and teach conflict resolution to his clients.

My own work life has been a history of progressively connecting more elements of myself into my work, reaching a true integration and power point in the "Rekindling the Spirit in Work" seminars. An important principle I have noticed in this process is that everything we do builds skills for the next step and the expression of our life purpose. For the most part, we do not have "wasted" jobs that count for nothing, (though in the moment it may feel that way). We are always learning and practicing skills, even hard to recognize ones, that move us forward.

My first job was a newspaper delivery boy in Detroit. I remember getting up very early on dark cold mornings and riding down the empty streets, by the yellow street lights, to deliver the morning *News*. It was wonderful and horrible. It was an adventure, I learned a lot, and it involved suffering. That experience has been a microcosm of my work life.

My next job was a summer spent working for the Wayne County Parks and Recreation Department on a tree cutting crew. The work was physically demanding. It built my confidence in my ability to take on a challenge and succeed. Later, in college, I had two jobs. One, was as a salesman in a clothing store called Camelot Brothers. It catered to the style conscious at the University of Michigan. I also washed dishes and bussed tables at a fraternity house for meals.

In the first job, I learned that working in a dead atmosphere was boring and depressing. I knew I could find something much more alive through which to earn my living. In the second job, it was clear, that even doing menial work can feel good, if I was in a place I liked with interesting people. Washing dishes, I became aware that work can be fun.

Where I really learned the foundational skills for my present work was outside the formal occupational sector, through sport. In team sports, I realized the deep satisfaction that comes from cooperation. I also felt the deleterious effect of intense competition. It taught me a great deal about leadership. Through individual sports, I learned patience, persistence, and focus. I also learned about relying on myself.

My next job brought these skills together for more intensive practice. I was Head Counselor at a summer camp. This job was equivalent to being an Operations Manager, for two months, for a total community of three hundred people. I became more skillful at human relations and leadership in that job.

After I finished graduate school, I did some college teaching. It was the early seventies and I was still a hippie. I wore shorts, a tie-dye T-shirt, brought my dog to campus, and met classes on the lawn in the summer and the cafeteria in the winter. The work felt right. Though I didn't have the concept at the time, I was beginning to sense that my life purpose involved teaching. That particular form didn't last long, as I was too unconventional for the administration. Besides, I didn't yet know enough about how to shape university teaching into an expression of my Gift.

After that, I took up work as a carpenter. I enrolled in a woodworking program at a Junior College to learn the trade. The Registrar had a difficult time with me because they never had a Ph.D. apply to the carpentry program, and they couldn't accurately reflect "highest previous education" on their Admissions form.

I made furniture in a converted garage next to my house and did house remodeling for three years. I learned to be an entrepreneur, and the wonder of working at home, with no boss, and no fixed hours. I'd work morning until night, and sometimes through the night when I had orders. Other days, when things were slow, I didn't work at all. I went to the beach and played Frisbee.

As a carpenter and wood worker, I did things I never thought I could do. My parents and teachers had convinced me I wasn't handy. Doing woodworking for a living blew that entire self-limiting definition apart. I loved the smell of the wood and the feel of it in my hands. Breaking out of this limitation and feeling the competence and confidence in my hands really opened me to take on challenges that at first seemed beyond me.

Then art came into my life. I read Walt Whitman and cried. I started writing poetry and moved to the beach in the same period. The poetry came out profusely in six books. It was as if I had a lifetime of poems stored up, and I let them all out at once.

From that came painting. Two friends helped me over the blocks that were keeping me from doing it. I always loved the idea of painting but I had believed every one else's story in my growing years that I wasn't artistic. I began to paint and it has been a passion that has served me for almost fifteen years now. I have made some money from painting sales, but mostly it has been a practice that has taught me how to handle the fire of creativity.

From painting and poetry, I learned to listen to my inner voice. This is the part of me that directs my next movement. The next word, the next brush stroke. It is the voice of intuition. Much of what I now do with groups and individuals is a result of learning that ability to listen for inner guidance about my next step. In the present, I express my creativity through people work and writing. Doing this work involves the same kind of energy and has the same feeling tone as poetry and painting .

Along the way, when I was about to become a father, I got a job with a research and consulting firm. I was running scared toward more income and security. I was happy to have a reliable and adequate paycheck. But I hated it. The firm survived on government contracts. The level of bullshit between people and with the client agencies was enormous. There were endless, boring, unproductive meetings. I had to get out. But, I learned some very important skills there which have served me well. Particularly, I became familiar with the ways of the non-profit agencies, an area of specialization in my present consulting practice.

In 1980, I left the consulting firm and opened my private practice. This was a major occupational shift. It happened synchronistically with another major shift in my life, my mother's death. In fact, my decision to go into this work was solidified through a conversation with my brother in the hospital cafeteria, where we waited for so long.

I chose to work with small organizations as a hands-on social psychologist. That made sense. My skill was in group work. I wanted to move out of the public sector, grants-based economy, where everything was fuzzy, into the private sector where I thought things would be more clear. Later, I found that this business, which I had "invented" in the hospital cafeteria, was a formal academic discipline called Organization Development. I worked hard to develop both the consulting skills and the business.

Two years later, I went to the California Institute of Integral Studies, in San Francisco, to take a meditation class. This began an association that resulted in becoming Professor of Organization Development and Transformation and Chairperson of the department at the Institute.

The magic of this association for me was that the Institute was the place where I learned to integrate my spiritual life and my work life. Before, I had my spiritual life and my work life in separate compartments. I meditated and studied religion and philosophy. And I did consulting. The two did not consciously meet.

After I began teaching at the Institute, I specialized in a subfield of Organization Development called Organization Transformation. This perspective focuses on spirit in the work place. It was a blessing for me because it gave me the opportunity to bring the most important parts of my life together in my work.

Then, at a workshop at Esalen, in Big Sur, California, I discovered individually-focused growth work, in the group setting. I had been working with organizations and groups as my focus for years. I went to Esalen with twenty other organizational consultants and participated in a psychosynthesis seminar. There I saw a master at work. Harry Sloan was able to evoke in each participant what he or she needed for the next step in their growth. His facilitation of the individual's process in the group setting was like a symphony conductor bringing forth the best performance from every player. I was deeply inspired by Harry, both the work that he did, and as a model of a man who put all of himself into his work.

I quickly gravitated toward this work. I studied it intensely and had a powerful natural talent for it. Acting as a guide in the process of evoking another's truth and as a healing agent in the release of emotional blocks has become my work.

Now, I am no longer at the Institute. I am fully engaged as a management consultant, seminar leader, teacher, and writer. Each step in this progression has been like adding another necessary square to what is now a fully developed quilt.

Integralism

Integralism is a term borrowed from the work of Sri Aurobindo, an Indian Teacher, whose approach was termed Integral Yoga. Integralism, to me, means the interweaving of all the constituent parts that make a balanced and complete whole. There are many ways to distribute the elements that make a complete whole. The Native Americans might say there are four: east, south, west, and north. The Chinese give five: earth, wood, water, fire, and metal. Other traditions might use fire, water, earth, and air.

The model that I see as the most helpful involves four elements: spirit, body, mind, and heart. Imagine a circle with spirit in the center; the originating central primary force. The other three elements, body, mind, and emotions can be understood as constituting a second circle around it. The following graphic simply presents this Integral Model.

Integral Model

Body, of course, represents the physical component of our being. Emotions represent our feelings, and Mind is the arena of thought. Spirit, in the center, is the originating force, the Great Mystery.

If we integrate all four of the elements into our lives and work, we can be balanced and happy. Integration means wholeness. The key to realizing spirit in work is bringing one's whole self to the effort. To realize spirit, one must also realize the body, mind, and emotions. The elements of mind and body are overly emphasized in western economic culture. The physical plant, the product, the bodies and ideas that sustain them are viewed as everything, and as a result, we are dangerously out of balance.

Because all four elements constitute an integrated system, if one element is adversely affected, the others will likely be depressed as well, for example, if you are emotionally troubled, it is likely to effect your physical body and your thinking process and spirit.

Using this same principle in reverse, you can positively effect all the other elements within you by affecting any one element. The system can be entered through the most convenient door. You can heal emotional wounding, for instance, through physical release. Numerous times, as a body work client, images of my childhood have come to mind, and I have released the emotional material into the hands of the practitioner.

Similarly, emotional release work, described in depth in Chapter Four, can have a powerful healing effect on the body. A woman with whom I worked in a "Rekindling the Spirit in Work" seminar, an artist, got in touch with a strong emotional block. She began to open up to powerful feelings in her body and discovered her rage at her husband for the lack of sexual passion in her life. The anger was locked in her pelvis. When she fully felt the pain and experienced the insight into its cause, her pelvis unlocked and the pain dissolved. She was able to think more clearly about her work and relationship and felt very uplifted in spirit. The willingness to experience the pain, both physically and emotionally, and to open to the insights it brings, can be a healing process for body, mind, and spirit.

Integration of Opposites

Reconciling apparently opposing forces is a concept central to integralism. Truth exists, at least partially, in all perspectives. While we may think and feel we have the truth, actually we have but one view. Others have their views. Each is valid from each unique perspective. Resolving conflict from an integral perspective involves the transformation of apparent opposites into a harmonious whole.

The philosophical underpinnings of this view is called, in the Hindu Vedantic tradition, advaita, or non-dualism. The non-dualist view is that all is one. There is no this and that, you and I, the fly I just killed and me. We are all one, part of a unitary fabric. In non-normal states of consciousness, like dreams or illness, this unity is sometimes apparent and very real.

From this perspective, all opposites are a result of illusion, the fruit of our conceptual framework, shaped by language. Our language is dualistic and so is our thought. So, the apparent contradictions we feel about work are not actually real. They are apparent contradictions shaped by our language and conceptual structure. When we move beyond these limitations, we see that we do not have contradictions in our desires around work, and that, in fact, they can all be integrated.

We can begin to open to the non-dualistic state, the state of no contradictions around work, by learning to allow the contradictions we do feel to be there — not to be closed to them or deny the feeling. This incongruity is critical. It is like not rejecting the rejection, to be in a state of acceptance.

Instead of believing we must choose between this or that, allow both. For instance, instead of choosing between the need for freedom and the need for security in work, let both needs coexist. Instead of choosing between the desire to work alone and the desire to work on a team, let them both exist. Drop the concept that there is a contradiction.

There are jobs that provide both team time and alone time. Jobs that provide freedom and security. Being free and being secure is not a contradiction. Being alone and being together is not a contradiction. Hold both.

> *Even if the flower fades it will be beautiful.*
> *Have you really observed a flower fading? It is beautiful.*
> *It has a sadness about it*
> *but who told you that sadness is not beautiful?*
> *Who says that only laughter is beautiful?*
> *I tell you that laughter is shallow if there is no sadness in it.*
> *And sadness is dead if there is not a smile in it.*
> *They are not opposites, they enrich each other.*[1]

If we do not close down on our feelings and hold open apparent contradictions about work, these "opposites" can integrate into a third option that may be entirely unexpected and unpredictable. The following exercise will provide an experience of this for you.

EXERCISE

Holding Both

- Be seated in a comfortable position. Allow yourself to relax. Bring your attention to the breath. Without any attempt to change it, simply focus on the breath, watching the natural rhythm of its in and out flow. Exhale any tension with the exhaling breath. Relax your whole body, section by section, from the feet to the head.

---

1. Bhagwan Shree Rajneesh, *When the Shoe Fits: Talks on the stories of Chuang Tzu,* Compilation; Swami Amrit Pathik, Editing; Ma Prem Veena, (The Rajneesh Foundation, Poona, India, 1976), p354.

- Allow yourself to let in an inner conflict you presently have about work. Slowly, giving everything lots of time, identify the different elements in the conflict.
- Let yourself focus your attention first on the feeling tone of one element. Allow the feeling in fully.
- Let a name arise for that part.
- Now, focus your attention on the feeling tone of the second element in the conflict. Allow the feeling tone in fully.
- Let a name arise for that part.
- Now, put one conflicting quality in each hand. Put your arms straight out in front of you and feel the qualities in each hand. Let your arms and hands move up and down, as if feeling the weight in each of them.
- Instead of choosing between the two, consider the possibility of holding both. Of letting them both be there without there having to be either a contradiction or a resolution.
- How does that feel?
- Now, let the two parts that are in your hands talk to each other and listen to each others' needs.
- Bring the two hands together and notice what insight arises.
- Be quiet and patient and give this process time. Let your mind be on holiday and allow the parts in your hands to integrate into one unified whole.
- When you are complete, return your attention to your breath, then your body. When you are ready, open your eyes.

This exercise can help dissolve apparent inner contradictions.

Dynamic Balance

Arriving at an end state is an illusion. Thinking we will once and for all achieve a perfect balance between all our integrated parts is also an illusion. It is a myth that we develop ourselves until we reach a point at which "we have it together." We never have it together, finally.

In the West we have also interpreted the Eastern concept of enlightenment erroneously. It is not an end state. These sacred traditions recognize that we humans can continue unfolding our poten-

tial even after attaining enlightenment because, while there is a per-
fection at the heart of all things, the human journey is one of continually unfolding levels of development.

The myths that "once we get it together, everything will be alright"
is harmful. Our life experience tells us that we always, and continually, reach upward. We achieve one level, perhaps plateau there a
while, and then another challenge arises, and through it, we move
forward again.

All of life is like this: continuing movement, dynamic balance.
Dynamic balance is a concept that assumes continuous movement.
Dynamic balance as a concept assumes that we never finally achieve
a steady state. The balance itself is always changing.

We can achieve balance in our work, but we cannot expect it to
stay the same. We cannot freeze-frame job satisfaction. It will continually change and we will have to continually adapt to remain
integrated. The exact nature of the balance moves. So, we can't ever
become complacent that we have found our perfect work and all
will be well for the rest of our lives. We must continue to stay aware
and flexible to make the necessary adjustments to move into balance and our power point.

The process of remaining current and keeping up with the dynamic character of our work life involves continuing to remain open
to the unfolding story told by our emotions and to the information
about our development and about what our next steps should be.

3 🌾 CREATING OUR WORK IN A "9 TO 5" SYSTEM

> *More will be accomplished, and better,*
> *and with more ease, if everyone does*
> *what he or she is best suited to do,*
> *and nothing else.*
>
> **PLATO**

There are two trends in the structure of the workplace. One is toward the mechanistic model, and the the other toward the organic. The mechanistic model treats the economic organization as a machine. The organic treats it as a living entity.

Presently, the mechanistic form is predominant. It is the "9 to 5," tightly structured system. It is designed to be an efficient machine. The individuals in it are seen as interchangeable parts. Like an engine, with standardized pistons and valves, they are not unique.

The mechanisitic form, which many of us try to fit ourselves into in order to earn our livlihood, is dehumanizing and alienating.

As we are each, at Essence level, reflections of the Divine, and, at the same time, completely unique, the interchangable parts model does not fit well. A system designed for non-interchangable, totally unique parts would be the appropriate fit for people at work.

Unfortunately, at this time, the mechanistic model dominates. Most organizations are structured in this way and do not support either our universality or our uniqueness.

The mechanistic system is not at an integral system. It does not nurture all levels of our being. The justification for the mechanical system is that it is the most efficient. It is not. Efficiency, the highest level of quality output given the limitations of the available resources, is best nurtured by supporting the whole person at work. The person who brings and uses all of themselves, the physical, emotional, mental, and spiritual aspects, is more effective, more efficient, and more productive than someone who only brings part of themselves to work.

Our mechanistic organizations do not get the highest level of quality output from the people working in them. Because people are not interchangeable parts, there is an incongruence between the mechanistic systems assumptions and the reality of the parts/people actually working in them.

Any craftsman knows that you cannot use inappropriate materials and produce a quality product. You cannot use coconut shells for making shoes. Similarly, people — organic, whole beings — with a need to be nourished at all levels are not the best fuel for driving the machines.

Perhaps robots are the perfect workers for our business organizations. Robots are the summation of interchangeable parts and appropriately suited for use in organizations based on the machine model.

I saw on the television the other day a program about work. They interviewed a woman who had grown up in a rural Indian village in South America. She had come to the city and was talking about her experiences. She said, "My life and my work are separate now. I go to work all day, and I come home. In order to fit in at work, I'm not the person I am at home. At work I don't give everything, I hold back. In the village where I came from, it was never like that. It was all the same. You put everything into your life. Here you have to choose whether you live or you work."

The mechanistic work organization, for many of us, is a kind of indentured servitude. D.H. Lawrence called it, "wage slavery." We sell ourselves for a paycheck. We perform fixed tasks, for a fixed number of hours, over a fixed number of days. Week in and week out, month in and month out, year in and year out, until we are too old to continue. This is not a context that supports our individual growth, nor does it support true economic productivity.

Like servitude, it creates powerful dependence. People are afraid to shift their work and move into work that is more supportive of who they are, and who they are becoming. Security becomes the foremost consideration. Essence and expressing our gift are less relevant.

There is an interesting section in James Clavell's novel, *King Rat*, that tells the story of Allied prisoners in a Japanese prisoner of war camp, in Singapore, during World War II. The prisoners evolve a lifestyle that is an adaptation to the horrible conditions. They hate their lives. Their friends are dying all around them, they are sick, weak, underfed, and hopeless. But, they have learned to adapt and survive.

When the first Allied troops roll in to liberate the camp at the war's end, there is no joy, only deadness and fear. The men became habituated to their degrading life style and were afraid to change. Also, they were so dehumanized by the system, their ability to respond at the emotional level was almost nonexistent. And, unbelievably, many did not want to leave the camp. They resisted their liberators. Some had to be forced to their freedom.

Presently, in the movement to shift the system of work from the old mechanistic form to the new humanistic organic form, people resist at all levels. Owners, managers, and workers. There is fear and deadness everywhere.

This is only fear of the unfamiliar. The way it is now is not working. Individuals in the system are getting sick at higher and higher rates. There is less satisfaction with work than ever. And, the corporate sector is becoming less efficient, less productive, and less profitable.

The mechanistic approach is just as harmful to those who own the businesses as it is to those who work in them. Wage slaves are not really creative, productive workers. They work mostly from fear, put out the least possible effort, and produce the minimum necessary to keep their positions. Their primary concern is individual survival, not group or organizational productivity. The mechanistic business organization is not only alienating to the individual, it is inefficient for the economy.

The system is crying out for change. The change that is most needed is to move toward the organic model of organization. From this perspective, organizations are treated as living entities, not dead machines. The metaphor is to plants and animals, not engines. The key feature of an organic organization is that, like people, it has various levels of being that need attending to if it is to operate at full potential.

An organic organization is an integral organization. It has parallel aspects to the physical, mental, emotional, and spiritual qualities of the human being. A business organization, if it is to be healthy and productive, as well as supportive of the growth and development of its workers, must attend to the well-being of the system at all levels. Attending to only one, two, or three is not enough. Mechanistic economic institutions tend to emphasize the mental and physical components of the organization. The physical plant, the bodies that drive it, and the ideas that run it are the focus of energy.

But there is also the heart and spirit of the organization to consider; the emotional tone of the business, and the spirit of its people. These need to be nourished and developed as well.

Mechanical model business organizations are no longer appropriate or adequate to compete in the world economy. With so little attention given to the emotional and spiritual components of the organization, they are not taking care of the full range of needs of their people. Organizations that are not organic and integral will not flourish. They are destined to live in disharmony and disease, and perish.

An integral organization recognizes all of its needs, including the full range of needs of its people. An integral organization finds ways, in an ever-changing manner, to achieve balance within each level, and across the four dimensions. In an integral business, the organization supports the health and growth of its people, and the people support the health and growth of the organization.

In the mechanical form which presently predominates, the people and their economic institutions are adversaries. Whether they like it or not, whether they want it or not, the owners and the bosses are the masters, and everyone else are the servants. It is an environment that kills the spirit in work.

The organic workplace, on the other hand, is a context that supports the expression of our Essence and our personal gifts. Any business in which its people are giving at the high level of quality commensurate with their uniqueness will be more effective, efficient, productive, and profitable than a indentured, driven organization. In an integral workplace, work is meaningful, and there is a fit between who we are and what we do.

The key to creating our own work within the "9 to 5" system is shifting our perspective from seeing work as something that someone gives us, to something we create. We shift from focusing on "getting a job," to creating our work.

The word "job," and our way of thinking about it, implies dependency. We "look for a job," "we find a job," "we get a job." It all implies that there is some fixed thing out there which we need, and someone else has it. Then, when we find it, they give it to us. We are the powerless recipients. The work we are doing is someone else's creation. They are in control. This perspective creates a subservient frame of mind.

The alternative is to see our work as our own creation. This doesn't mean that we must all be entrepreneurs or independent professionals. We may work in a "job," or be employed in an organization, but it will be one that we have chosen, because it fits who we are and allows us to express our uniqueness. We will have chosen a job because its a form in which we can forward our life purpose. We are not simply giving ourself to an employer for a paycheck, we are accepting the fit between the employer's need and our need, for mutual benefit.

The important distinction is to shift from an emphasis on "job" to a focus on life work. The jobs may change, the form of employment may change, but the life work, or our expression of Essence and our gift, continually evolves and grows.

We do not have to jump at jobs to earn our livlihood. We can take the slower, more certain approach of building our work. There are many jobs that fit into this creative process. As the great Sufi poet Jalaladin Rumi wrote, "There are a thousand ways to kneel and kiss the earth."

It is better to take our time, be clear on our direction and purpose, foster courage and patience in the face of insecurity, and select work opportunities that support us in being all of who we are.

It is important to fully understand that like any significant creation, making it takes time. It is useful to see ourselves as one of the "Old Masters." First we prepare ourselves, learning the necessary skills to execute our work. Then we work in ways that build our skills and develop our experience. Finally, we can fully express our uniqueness and originally, as independent Masters.

Building our work, rather than just "taking a job," is a slower, long-term process. It takes patience and perspective, particularly at the front end. However, in the long term, it is more dynamic, interesting, and rewarding than a life full of "jobs." It requires the self-control to not jump after a pay check and get stuck in a job that is not right for you.

I notice that many of my students who complete their graduate studies have the expectation that they will immediately "get a job" doing exactly what they want to do. It is a perspective that assumes career is not a growing evolutionary process, but more like a Christmas present, comes all at once, nicely wrapped. This belief is like Michealangelo thinking he would receive the commission for the Sistine Chapel as soon as he completed Art School.

It is not that we should always be holding out for work that is the "perfect," final expression of who we are. The process is developmental. We are building and creating. But we are not, except in the case of emergencies, and for short periods, "getting a job" as indentured servants that does not take us towards where we want to go.

It takes many years to develop our work. It cannot, and should not, be rushed. Unfortunately, few people have the patience and fortitude to create their work. Instead, they take the fast track, finding a job and staying in it. Sometimes they get fed up, quit their job, and then take another, but without building or growing their life purpose. This approach yields only a short-run pay off and can have disastrous long-term consequences. The "taking a job" model can turn into an apparent dead end while creating your work grows forever.

The creation process requires vision. What is your dream? Who are you, and what do you have to contribute? This is the work of discovering Essence and identifying your gift discussed in Chapters One and Two. When we are in touch with our Essence and our Gift, the direction in our work becomes clear.

If we make a commitment to create our work as an expression of who we are, and if we have the patience and courage to stay with it, we will succeed, even in the mechanistic environment.

With vision, courage, and patience, the individual can triumph. We can all do work that satisfies us, frees our spirit, and feeds our needs at all levels. Nobody gives us that, we create it. Like a painter painting a landscape, a gardener growing a garden, or an architect building a building, we construct each element. The foundation is training, the lower floors are skill building and experience, the upper stories are our unique creative contribution.

Kahil Ghibran said, "Work is love made visible." Work is too central and too important to leave to the "job market" to determine for us. We must be intimately and energetically involved in constructing it. Creating our work is expressing our love in the world. And, just as it takes time to learn to love gracefully and well, so does it take time to learn to express ourselves through our work.

The following exercise follows upon previous insights developed in Chapters One and Two and will help you clarify your next steps in creating your work.

EXERCISE

Visualizing Your 'Perfect' Work

- Lie down or be seated in a comfortable position. Allow yourself to relax. Bring your attention to the breath. Without any attempt to change it, simply focus on the breath, watching the natural rhythm of its in and out flow. Exhale any tension with the exhaling breath. Relax your whole body, section by section, from the feet to the head.

- Now, bring in the affirmation you developed earlier. Let it sink in deeply. Allow your body to really open to the feeling tone that comes with it.

- In this deep inner state of relaxation, go to a place in nature, in your "mind's eye," where you feel comfortable, safe, and secure.

- Take that place in deeply. See things clearly, as if you are focusing a camera to a very clear image.

- Take in the scene with your other senses. Smell the smells and hear the sounds.

- Remind yourself of your unique gift that you have been giving, and will continue to give, to the world and the people around you.

- Know that from an identification with Essence, and the knowledge of your gift, you will now take a journey to reveal more information about the "perfect" work for you.

- Notice that in the distance is a tunnel. A tunnel that feels support-ive to your gaining deeper knowledge about yourself. It may be a tunnel of tree boughs, of flowers, or a tunnel of earth and rock.
- Now slowly walk through the tunnel, leaving the everyday world behind.
- On coming out the other side, see yourself in your "perfect" work, in your "perfect" work environment. Don't "think," just allow infor-mation to come to you about your life's work and the steps to manifesting it. Just allow this to unfold slowly and easily. It is not necessary to "try."
- Open to the impressions, insights, and feelings.
- After about five minutes, when you feel the time is right, return through the passage of the tunnel, and rest in that beautiful place on the other side.
- As a transition, return your attention to the breath. Now, move into your body. Feel your body. Your bottom, and back and hands. Get a good sense of returning to wakeful consciousness.
- Open your eyes when you are ready, and write down what you learned.

II

WORK

4 🌿 FEELING THE FEELINGS
INTEGRATING THE DARK SIDE

The way out is through
ANONYMOUS

It is not possible to live in a state of Essence without continually integrating the parts of ourselves that block our ability to identity at that level. The blocks come in the form of thoughts, emotions, and feelings, states that move us away from identification with Essence and into identification with a sub-personality.

Thoughts are objects of the mind. Emotions are objects of the heart, and feelings are objects of the body. Thought is experienced as occurring in the mind. Emotions are mythically seeded in the heart and are a more generalized state, like sadness, when compared with feelings that are specific sensations in the body, like tightness in the stomach.

For instance, when we feel afraid about changing jobs, begin to identify ourselves unconsciously with the fear; we become the fear. We don't often experience our feelings as partial components of ourselves, as temporary experiences. Rather we become the feeling. What is experienced is "I am fear." We identify with the fearful sub-personality and forget our true nature. A correct description of the situations would be, "I have this fear, but I am not this fear; I am Essence."

Denying that we have blocks to identifying with Essence is not effective. The blocks contain information we need in order to grow. They will continue to arise until we listen. Our emotions are the source of information that guide us in the process of clearing past wounding and allowing blocks to dissolve. Feelings, or the body sensations associated with thoughts and emotions, hold the key to our next steps toward wholeness and freedom. If we can learn to open to our feeling states, we have a direct line to the information necessary for our personal and occupational growth.

There is an old Hindu story of an Indian man who spent his entire life in search of happiness. He never found it. In fact, quite the opposite, he was one of the most unhappy people in his small village in southern Madras.

Then, one day, on his seventy-fifth birthday, everyone noticed he became happy. His friends were mystified, they said, "Pravin, what has happened to you? You have been unhappy for seventy-five years and now you are completely changed." The old man replied, "I worked my whole life at being happy and I could not achieve it, so I gave up. I said to myself, seventy-five years wasted, now I will just do without happiness. In that moment, I became happy."

The story illustrates the need to let go of our desperate seeking after happiness, our clinging to feeling good, and opening to the discomfort, so that through it we can become happiness. Most of the time we are so attached to feeling good that we do not allow, accept, or acknowledge the feelings we are actually having. We don't open to our difficult and uncomfortable feelings. We push them away, with the result that the precious truth they contain is lost.

Feeling states represent information that is trying to emerge. As we discussed in Chapter One, our personal affirmation is often a word that represents the aspect of Essence growing in the present. Our feeling states are also parts of ourselves emerging in the present. They carry the information we need in the moment to clear the restrictions of old wounding and open up the inner space in which Essence can reside.

It is very partial, very incomplete, to seek after happiness through pushing away pain. This approach will have the opposite effect. It will keep us in a state of unhappiness by keeping us stuck with our history of identification with sub-personalities and not allow identification with Essence, from which happiness can emerge.

Feelings are like stories held in the body. If we begin to feel the feelings in the body, the stories emerge. The way to listen to and learning from these stories is straightforward. When we notice a strong feeling coming out of an emotional state or a thought pattern, we stop and focus our awareness on the feeling. This may be at the time the feeling state arises, or, if that is not possible due to the practical considerations of the moment, later when we have a private moment.

Once our attention is totally focused on the feeling, information will begin to emerge. Images and words will arise. If we stay with those images and words, progressively dropping deeper into the feeling tone in our body, then more information will be forthcoming.

Usually, the information that comes to us will move progressively backward toward our past. We may be feeling anger in the present, at our boss, but when we stay with the feeling we find words, images, and information related to previous injuries caused by encounters with authority. As the story from the feelings continues to unfold, we may even get to the historical root of the present feeling in a past experience.

The root usually lies in our childhood, at a point when some "shock" to our system occurred. Shocks are powerful negative events in our lives that cause constrictions within us and freeze our emotional development around matters related to that experience. If my father exerted his authority painfully upon me, it is likely that some of the occasions in which that happened will have shocked my system and frozen my emotions around authority at the level of reaction I had to my father at that time. As Reshad Feild, a contemporary teacher in the Sufi tradition, has said, "Shock, acting as a wound, helps to produce blocks in our lives which then may cause us to over-compensate. Moments of shock can steal a portion of our senses which then remain locked in the pattern. Until those frozen pieces of ourselves are redeemed and healed, we cannot be completely in the present moment. If we are not totally here with all of our being, we are not fully alive and thus are limited in the development of our full potential."[1]

If I wish to come into a more positive and appropriate relationship to authority, then I must open to my feelings, and the information they bring me,when I feel strongly about issues related to au-

1. Reshad Feild, *Here To Heal*, Element Books, Longmead, Shaftesbury, Dorset, England, 1985, pages 48 and 61.

thority. When I have reactions to my boss, if I wish to have some control over how I relate to him rather than to be enslaved to the patterns I took on at the time of my original shocking, I need to open to the insights and emotional release that focusing on the feelings will bring.

When we put our full awareness on our uncomfortable feelings, our pain, the material this process produces — words, images and insights — can release old shocks that have frozen our development and allow us to make free choices in the present. We can create the freedom within ourselves to make constructive choices about work by facing the pain of the feelings we have.

Recently, I felt guilty that I wasn't working harder at my university job and my writing — in fact, at most everything I do — household chores, preparing for clients meetings, and so on. Yet, as my partner Barbara reminded me, I often do a full days work "before breakfast."

So, I sat quietly and focused my attention on the feelings in my body that accompanied this guilt. I began to feel a strong sensation in my upper chest. It was an unusual feeling that I couldn't identify. Then, slowly, it came to me that it was a feeling of "empty heaviness." This was a paradox I had never encountered or even thought of, "empty heaviness." To my logical mind, these qualities don't go together, but it was an exact description of how I was feeling. As I stayed with the feeling and these words, I saw a round image that was both an air balloon and a heavy ball. Empty as air and heavy like steel, both at the same time.

Using a method discussed later in the chapter, I began a dialogue with the image and asked "What's going on?" The information that came to me was, "You're trying to be perfect. You're trying to be everything and it's not necessary." I then asked the image "Who am I trying to satisfy, "The response from the image was "Your mother, the people around you, your new partner at work."

My body immediately relaxed. Reflexively, I took a deep, releasing breath. I had uncovered an important insight that was driving the discomfort of guilt, and I was beginning to be free of it. At the time, I was hiring a new faculty member, and I had been tense trying to impress her with my competence; that I am capable of living up to her expectations. Though technically she works for me, because I was frozen in an old pattern of pleasing my mother through pleasing other women in my life, I was still being driven in the present to prove to this woman that I am good enough and worthy of love.

What a great relief it was to see this and how it was holding me back in my present life. What a joy it was to be free of the guilt. I felt light and free inside. The problem was not that I had not been working hard enough; it lay in a deeper invisible shock and pattern of restriction around pleasing women. Working harder would have been of no help. I needed to do the inner work of listening to the story locked in my feelings in order to move beyond its limitations. We can't go around the blocks to Essence, we can only go through them.

Work and Our Emotional Life

Challenge yourself with the thought that work itself is not a complex matter. It is rather a straightforward question of earning a livelihood at something that fits with who we are. But you are probably reading this book because finding the right work seems a very complex and confusing matter.

Consider the possibility that your work itself is not causing you difficulties, it is the emotions you feel about it that are the problem. Work is not complex, it is how we feel about work that is difficult and confusing. The way to effectively deal with our concerns about work, then, is to skillfully deal with our emotions.

What does it mean to be skillful with our emotions? For the most part, it is exercising the courage to stay with the feelings our emotions bring, which are painful or unpleasant, and open to their story.

Thich Nhat Hahn, a wonderful Vietnamese teacher in the Buddhist tradition, speaks of the "liberation of understanding." When we are willing to focus our awareness on our inner feelings, it is like the sun shining on a closed flower. The warmth allows the flower to open with its gift to the world. Through the warmth of our focused attention, the insight of the emotion is yielded. This is the "liberation of understanding." Nothing else is needed; no action, no change, is demanded; only the simple willingness to stay with the feeling; the liberation of understanding will naturally emerge.

When feelings of confusion or discomfort come up regarding work, instead of first trying to figure out a course of action to change the outer situation to one that will theoretically will make me "happy," the skillful behavior is first to drop fully into the feeling state. Stay with the feeling tone in the body. Open to the information it yields and then construct actions in the world based upon this new insight.

When one first begins this process, it is striking how "old and familiar" the feelings seem. We have been experiencing and re-experiencing the same feelings all our lives, in various domains, including work, because we have not listened to their message. When we listen, the emotions and feelings no longer need to emerge. New ones appear, of course, but they serve to heal wounds lying still deeper, until, as time goes on, and feeling work proceeds, we begin to be free of the frozen patterns of our shocks, and able to live with flexibility in the present, in Essence.

The healing process for feelings is similar to the healing process for the body. Signals arise naturally out of the body telling us that something is wrong. The pain is a communication from the body to the mind that one of its parts needs attention. Imagine what would happen if we hurt our body badly and paid no attention to it, as we often do with our feelings. We are preparing dinner, for instance, and suddenly we cut our finger badly. We immediately feel the pain and see the blood, but because we are hungry and don't want to deal with it, we cuss and stop the blood flow with the closest available rag. We continue to prepare the food, as if nothing has happened, yet all the time in pain. We try, possibly successfully, to keep our mind occupied with thoughts so that our awareness is dimmed.

In this scenario we are likely to do damage to our body that could have been avoided by listening to its message. The finger will not heal quickly or well, leaving us free to work with ease unless it is well attended. Similarly, we must attend our emotional pain when it cries out for attention.

When we are feeling dissatisfaction in work, thinking first of changing jobs, doing an action in the external world in search of some illusory happiness, is not the best solution. The problem, the dissatisfaction, resides on the inside, and it is there it must be addressed. If we do not, we will simply recreate the dissatisfaction on the next job. Many of us have experienced this same phenomena in relationships. When we begin a new relationship, without having addressed the inner dynamics that ended the old one, it is likely we will recreate the same painful feelings again.

Denial, Addiction, and Work

Denial is the state of unwillingness to face our inner truth. It is a state of perpetual darkness because the light lies in the truth of our feelings. In denial, we cannot learn from our experience and shed our pain, because we are not willing to open to it's direction.

Addiction is a behavior pattern of habitual denial that takes us away from our feelings and their truth. Though I have my own gnawing addictions, I cannot claim to be an expert in the area. It is clear to me, however, that all addictions, in one way or another, are patterns that take us out of the feeling state we are in and transport us into another one which we think will make us feel good. Alcohol, drugs, gambling, over-work are all addictive behavior patterns that suppress how we feel and take us to another feeling state.

"Workaholism" is a way to not feel our feelings. We can bury ourselves in the doing of our work and avoid feeling the underlying emotions that would otherwise come up. Workaholism is an insidious and difficult addiction because hard work is so highly valued and well rewarded in our culture. Nonetheless, overwork can stunt our growth, keep us emotionally immature and ultimately in more pain than if we were willing to experience the pain of our feelings and work through them.

I know that I can successfully shut out all anxiety for a time by sitting at my desk and doing "busy work." But, the bigger and more important questions about my work will go unattended. I may appear to be doing my work, but what is really happening is I'm getting away from it. I am stifling the process of integration, of being all of who I am in work.

The other day, I had a strong drive to do something to change my mood. I could have gone to the desk and started writing immediately, and powered my way over the top of my discomfort, suppressing my feelings by throwing myself into another set of feelings. Or I could have looked for a way to change my mood through running, drinking a coffee, or smoking a cigarette. But, because I am writing this book and very involved with the work of staying with feelings, I had the willingness to sit with them, just as they were, without attempting to change them.

When I focused my attention on the actual feelings in my body, I noticed a light sensation in my head. Keeping my attention on that sensation for a short time an image emerged of a Court Jester or Fool; a medieval character with a triangular hat, various colored balls hanging from the edges and a red baggy suit. I stayed with that image and opened to the feeling tone of it. Internally, I asked the image, "What do you want?," and the words that came to me were "I want to have fun."

This simple piece of information was very useful. It took the feelings out of the moralistic realm of what I "should or shouldn't" do and made it very clear that this drive to change my mood was a life-supporting message being expressed to move me towards behaving kindly towards myself. When I realized this, there was no need to seek any outside stimulation. I knew how to have fun. Ultimately, I did the same thing I would have done without feeling my feelings, but which would have left me without the release from my emotional constriction. With great joy and a sense of freedom, I sat down and continued this book.

The "How To" of Feeling Release Work

There are direct and uncomplicated ways to access the information contained in our feelings. Focusing on the feeling tone in the body and allowing associations, words, and images to emerge is the most direct and simple method. One can then choose to engage in an inner dialogue with the image or the place in the body that is experiencing the strongest sensation to get yet a deeper level of insight.[2]

---

2. This approach is a synthesis of the "Focusing" method of Eugene Gendelin,

Engaging in this process is usually experienced as a subtle to strong release, or to use the psychological term, a catharsis. Bound up emotional energy, which has been trapped in the body, is dissipated, creating a sense of greater inner space and expanded freedom.

Psychosynthesis, as an integrated perspective, holds that all parts of our personality, our sub-personalities, originally developed with the positive function of taking care of us. The part of us that is very closed off to others, for instance, may be the part of us that originally protected us from abusive adults when we were children. Many of the sub-personalities have evolved as methods of self-protection. At one time or another, all of our sub-parts within the personality structure were useful to us.

As we grow into maturity and our circumstances change, some of these parts are not longer necessary, but they are still with us. It is as if they are stuck in a gear that worked in a previous period but is no longer the appropriate gear to be in now. In fact, being stuck in the wrong gear can be troublesome and dangerous.

Our feelings come up again and again so that we can be present and operating in the right gears, the ones that are appropriate for us now. The feelings come up so that they can be felt, addressed and released.

The other day, I was on a bicycle ride with three friends on a beautiful mountain trail near my home. I was pedalling easily and with great joy when I suddenly noticed that my friends were considerably ahead of me. Without being fully conscious of it, I got anxious. I became tense in the body and lost the feeling of great ease I had been experiencing. I started pedaling faster and harder. As my legs tightened up, I began to tire. As I noticed what was happening, I "woke up," decided to slow down, and look into the feelings I was experiencing.

I continued to peddle, but I turned my attention inward. When I opened to the feeling that was most prominent, I realized that the

---

the dialogue approach of the Gestalt therapist Fritz Perls, and the Psychosynthesis processing of Harry Sloan. See Eugene Gendelin, *Focusing,* Everest House, New York,1978. And Frederick Perls, Ralph Hefferline, Paul Goodman, Dell Publishing Company, New York, 1965.

Also, Roberto Assagioli, *Psychosynthesis,* The Viking Press, New York, 1965.

competitive part of me did not like being behind. That part of me wanted to catch up, in fact, pass those turkeys and ride first. When the information is that clear, even I can see the humor.

I laughed. All this anxiety because I still want to be first. As I stayed with the feeling, I saw its origin in my childhood and adolescence. I was a competitive athlete and it was very important to me to be first. That was how I stood apart from others. That was how I got acknowledgment, recognition, and strokes. A big part of my identity in those years was as a successful athlete.

Now, however, I'm not a competitive athlete. I'm a jogger and a bike rider and I do it for the simple pleasure of exercise and the outdoors. I don't need to be first. It is, in fact, irrelevant to my present identity and who I am now. When I saw this, my legs softened, I breathed deeply, and I released the body constriction that had tightened me up. I began to ride again with pleasure and ease.

Still, I knew there was more information, and I went further into the feeling I had been experiencing earlier and understood that the desire I had to compete has the feeling tone I sometimes experience when I am in the presence of a "star" in my field, or even with a colleague who is doing very well. I had previously experienced this feeling state as some sort of perversity that I was not happy that someone else was doing well. I criticized myself for feeling this way. Because of the self-judgement, it felt so bad that I didn't stay with the feeling. I skidded off it, and never understood its deeper meaning. There was a harsh, uncomfortable tone to the feeling that I recognized on the bicycle ride as the same one I had on the basketball court, or the baseball diamond, or the track. I wanted to be outstanding, and to the extent that others were also, it diminished the light shining on me.

So the pattern was becoming clear, as well as its effect on my life. As a youth I wanted to be first in sports. As an adult, I have carried this drive into leisure activities, and my work. I don't want others out in front of me, and when they are, I feel bad and try my hardest to catch up.

Now, with the help of this insight, I can choose to use my competitive edge to drive me forward in my work, or I can choose to release this discomfort and trust that coming from Essence is my path to excellence in work. I am now free to choose instead of helplessly trapped in the discomfort of a frozen pattern. I am choosing to release the competitive sub-personalities, even in my work, and it feels right. It feels lighter and more free.

There are specific steps we can take to access our feelings, learn from their information, and release the constrictions that hold us back. Below is a simple generic approach to experiencing the "liberation of understanding." Following this is a specific exercise to guide you into the experience.

1. Pay attention when thoughts or an emotional state are manifesting as strong feelings.

2. Allow the feelings to be there without denial, pushing them away or avoiding them.

3. Progressively open more fully to the feeling, notice the place in your body where the physical sensation is most prominent.

4. Letting go of the focus on the thoughts or emotions themselves, focus all your attention on the physical sensation.

5. Amplify the feeling tone. Let it get bigger.

6. Step in and "become the feeling."

7. With your mind and thoughts "on holiday," allow a word or image to "bubble up" to you, directly from that place in your body.

8. If you get an image, consider that the image is a symbol of the sub-personality that is creating this feeling and:

    a. Internally ask the symbol what it wants. Let the symbol, not your mind, reply.

    b. Now ask it what it really, really needs, and let the symbol reply.

9. If a symbol doesn't come to you, use the physical place and ask that place what it wants. Then ask it what it really needs.

10. When you receive the information from the symbol, or from your body, really allow your whole self to soak it in. Go slowly and relax. Allow spontaneous deep breathing to occur. This is a sign that it has reached the body level of understanding.

11. Allow the image or body part that is representative of a sub-personality to speak to the bigger part of you, your Essence

self, and ask it to see this smaller part's need for what has been identified above.

12. Then gracefully shift into an identification with Essence by using your affirmation and acknowledging from that identification that the need is seen and understood.

13. Allow a dialogue to develop between the sub-personality that has the need, and Essence, which sees and understands it.

This is a very healing process. It releases emotional constrictions, stuck thought patterns, and chronically uncomfortable feelings. It can get at the root cause of the feelings and allow their release.

The key is to understand the need of the sub-personality. The sub-part remains alive in our psyche because it has an unmet need. Discovering the need, acknowledging the need, and listening to it, produces the "liberation of understanding." The opening of the flower.

The following exercise is designed to give you an even more directed experience of the emotional release process.

EXERCISE

Finding the Deeper Need in the Emotional Block

- Be seated in a comfortable position. Allow yourself to relax. Bring your attention to the breath. Without any attempt to change it, simply focus on the breath, watching the natural rhythm of its in and out flow. Exhale any tension with the exhaling breath. Relax your whole body, section by section, from the feet to the head.

- Bring in the affirmation you developed in the exercises from Chapter One. Be with that affirmation. Repeat it slowly, allowing time between repetitions for the body to open up to the message.

- Notice when there is a block or resistance to easily affirming and accepting the affirmation.

- Focus your attention on the block. Allow the feeling fully in.

- Notice where in your body you feel it most. Put all your attention on that spot. Let it become all of who you are.

- Now, detaching your mind, as if it were on vacation, let the body itself speak to you. Let it "bubble up" words to your consciousness that describe the essential feeling you are experiencing in that body part.

- Ask that part in your body, "What do you want?" Wait patiently for your body to respond with an answer.

- Now ask your body, "Underneath that want, what do you really, really need?" Wait for an answer.

- Now, let that body part speak that need it has identified to your Essence. Let it say **See my need for**_____(filling in the blank with the information you have received).

- Now, with fluidity, become your Essence again by speaking your affirmation to yourself. When you feel identified with Essence, let it speak to the part with the need by saying **I see your need for**_____ (filling in the blank).

- Speak this request for seeing the need and responding to it two or three times. Then, let any dialogue develop that comes naturally between the part and the Essence.

- When we face our emotions directly, feel them, and allow ourselves to receive their information, the pain and fear we so often experience become the doorways to inner freedom and identification with Essence.

Working With The Voice Of The "Critic"

The "Critic" is a term widely used in popular psychology that refers to the part of ourselves that is self-critical. Actually, there is no one Critic. There are various sub-personalities, whose various voices manifest as what we are calling the unified Critic.

The part of me that was critical when I was falling behind bike riding was the voice of my competitive sub-personality. The part of me that determined I was not working hard enough, was the perfectionist sub-personality. Our Critic is not one entity that can be dealt with as a separate thing. We have various parts with various needs that manifest as a critical voice. If we are to proceed beyond self-criticsm into self-love, we will need to address each feeling state as it comes up in its full uniqueness. Defining all our blocks and critical voices as one voice will short-circuit the process of gathering the information we need to release the critical voices, one at a time.

I worked with a woman in a "Rekindling the Spirit in Work" seminar who was having great difficulty opening to an identification with Essence. Each time she tried to do so, a voice came to her, "This is baloney, you're not a Star, your just a regular person and don't give yourself airs." She told me, "My critic is keeping me down." She wasn't experiencing any release from the block to identifying with Essence, simply labeling the block as the Critic, and going no further. It served, in fact, as a diversion and excuse from doing the emotional clearing.

I worked with her on getting in touch with the body part that the feeling of the Critic resided in, and she got some important information about her childhood. Her father didn't want her to stand out. He often criticized her for "putting on airs," thinking herself a "big shot." As a result, Janice developed a protective sub-personality that did not allow her to think of herself as important. It had helped to minimize the verbal abuse of her father.

Now, as an adult whose father had long since passed on, the affirmation of Star, which came up for her in the Essence exercise, was in conflict with that protective sub-personality developed many years ago. When Janice got in touch with the part that had to be small to survive, she found that presently it needed "recognition." She worked with that and found she could recognize herself, and stand unafraid to be her true nature, the Star.

Its important not to lump all our blocks and voices into one category, naming it our Critic. We need to understand that we have many voices and many critics, all calling out with needs, and that to release them, we must address each one in its full uniqueness.

The "Organizing Principle"

With close attention we can trace the cause of our behavior from our action in the outer world to its roots in a deeper inner source. Often we do things, and later fit an explanation to the behavior that stands as a reason for its having occurred. For instance, we get angry at a co-worker and we say it's because they didn't treat one of our client's well. Yet somewhere inside we know that this reason feels partial, not fully true, almost inauthentic. It is as if the deeper cause of our behavior is not visible, we are not in touch with it, so we construct an explanation that seems to make sense out of what we feel or do.

For example, we may notice a pattern developing within us that we are not doing our job well. We are not attending to our responsibilities, we are getting sloppy and letting things slip. We may say to ourselves and others that we are tired or overwhelmed or not trained for the job. But deeper down lies the real source. We are bored and fed up with this job. We are afraid to quit for all the reasons all of us are afraid to change jobs. Yet if we consistently do our work poorly, we may get fired. Unconsciously, this may be a strategy for getting out of our job without quitting.

To be in more control of our worklife, we need to drop the belief in our easy explanations for our behavior and look more deeply into its real sources, which may not be immediately accessible. The process for getting in touch with the source of our behavior is similar to the feeling work described above.

This can be understood through a model developed by Harry Sloan, a brilliant psychosynthesis practitioner who lived and practiced in San Francisco until his death in 1988. Harry contended that we can understand human consciousness as having three levels. The outer layer is behavior, action in the world. The middle layer consists of attitudes that shape that behavior; like the attitude of prejudice driving the behavior of segregation. The deepest level, the causal level, is the "organizing principle." This is the source level for both attitudes and behavior. To understand the real reason for a behavior, or patterns of behaviors, we must understand the organizing principle from which they arise.

In our example, segregation arises from prejudice. Prejudice arises from the organizing principle, deep in our psyche, of self-hatred, developed in us by harsh parental criticism and projected by us onto others whom we perceive to be in a position weaker than us.

Because the organizing principle lies deep within us and is generally developed from seeds planted long ago, we are not often consciously aware of it. Usually, when we try to understand the cause of our behavior, at best, we drop into the attitude layer and locate the roots there. On my bike ride, for instance, I could have made up any number of reasons, and I often do, as to why I wanted to catch up with my friends; its more fun to ride with others, I need to get home to do the laundry, it might start raining, etc. But at the core, the organizing principle that motivated my behavior to increase my speed was the desire to be first. When I understood the organizing principle, I was able to release the behavior. It is difficult to release either the behavior or the attitude without releasing the organizing principle that drives it all.

It is through the feeling work we have described that we travel into the realm of the organizing principle and understand it. This opens the possibility for true understanding of the attitude system that emanates from the principle and drives the action. We can trace the real cause of behavior, then, by observing the outside layer and deducing the source through close attention to our feelings.

"Ripeness"

Sometimes we are ready to release our restricting feelings and sometimes we are not. This has been very noticeable to me in working with others to facilitate their disolution of emotional blocks. Some people are so obviously ready it seems that if a slight wind were to brush them lightly, they would be in direct contact with their core. Others are so obviously closed, guarded, defended, and not ready, that the mention of addressing underlying feelings is threatening.

This can be understood in terms of the organic metaphor of "ripeness." When the fruit is ripe, it is ready to be picked. When we are ready, we will release. Just as different fruits are in different stages of ripeness at different times, so are we. When we are in the green stage, we are not ready for picking. When we are in the ripe phase, or the over-ripe phase, we almost ooze out.

Annete was an attorney practicing family law. She was bright and sensitive. Working with families in the crisis of divorce was hard on her. But she felt loyal to her clients and was afraid to let go of the security of a profitable private practice. "This work is really tearing me up," she said. Annete was one of the few clients I have worked with that clearly needed to make a major change in her work. She was way out of line with who she truly is.

However, the time was not right. She wasn't ripe. Even the tone Annette used to speak her confusion was flat and cold; almost frozen, devoid of emotion. And Annette didn't move through her blocks to make a change. It wasn't her time, she wasn't ready. Annete alone, and we together, were not able to create the moment in which she could open to the source of her blocks and release them.

So we dropped it. Another time will come when she is ripe and ready, and she will take her appropriate next steps.

Conversely, Mary, another client, a salesperson and student, was completely ripe. She awoke on the second morning of the seminar with great sadness. As we sat in the circle, she was slumped, almost rolled in a ball. Soon she was fidgeting, sighing, almost crying out for help. She was clearly ripe and ready. I simply asked her how she was, and with very little intervention on my part, she did one half-hour of deep feeling release work.

Continuous Work

This is not the kind of process we can do "once and for all" and expect that we are clear and no longer have emotional blocks to satisfying work. We have created blocks throughout our life as reactions to shocks from numerous and varied sources. Releasing is an on-going practice over a lifetime. There is no therapy nor therapist that can keep up with the amount of emotional processing there is for us to do. Working with therapists and "guides" is very helpful, but self-work is the only way to do the amount of clearing we really require to live and work from Essence.

It is like the poet and storyteller Robert Bly's emphasis on the universal wisdom of fairy stories that depict the descent into the darkness of the underground. By going down into the darkness below and facing the demons in order to conquer them through understanding, we return more whole. Descent into the feeling realm, for Bly, is the key to ascension, and unification with Essence.

5 ⚜ THE POWER OF TRUTH

The nearer one approaches the Truth,
the happier one becomes.
For the essential nature of Truth is positive Absolute Bliss.

SIVANANDA

Truth-telling is an important vehicle for healing ourselves and our relationships with others in the workplace. It is a primary instrument for improving our own work life, the condition of the work group we are in, and the organization that employs us. The most difficult challenge of the truth-telling process is learning how to tell the truth to ourselves.

Most of us spend our lives on an illusive journey in search of happiness. Sadly, very few of us find it. I believe that if we make happiness our goal, we will not find it. If we seek truth, however, we may attain to happiness. Happiness is an outcome of other ways of being, it is not a state that itself can be directly achieved.

Truth, on the other hand, is a process and a way of being. We can "do truth," by having the courage to open to, and directly face, the reality of what we are thinking and feeling in the moment. We can seek and learn to be truthful with ourselves. The more we do this, as the sage Sivananda states in the introductory quote, the happier we will become.

Truth is the foundation for the emotional release work discussed in Chapter Four. To release a difficult feeling, we must first summon the courage to acknowledge that the pain is there and open ourselves to feeling it. This is the process of truth-telling with ourselves.

Often, however, we do not open to the truth of our pain. We avoid the reality of our feelings through countless efforts to minimize the discomfort. To do this we employ the psychological defense mechanisms of rationalization, avoidance, projection and so on. This is the process of non-truth-telling with ourselves, also termed denial.

Denial, or the consistent unwillingness to face the truth of our thoughts and feelings, is widespread in our lives. With its dominance, we cannot release the constrictions that bind us, and we cannot be in clear relationship to Essence. If we are in denial about our thoughts and feelings around work, work will not be an expression of Essence. It will be empty and dull. It will be a part split off from the rest of our lives, a dull drudgery through which we sacrifice ourselves to survive.

Facing the truth of our thoughts and feelings makes it possible to be free. And, speaking the truth of our thoughts and feelings to others creates the possibility of deep and rewarding connections with them. It keeps the air clean with our workmates and friends, so that our actions are in the present and authentic.

For many of us, particularly men, simply recognizing that we have a feeling, in order to open to the truth it holds, is difficult. And, it is impossible to open to the truth of our inner process if we cannot feel the process in the first place. Men in our culture have been encouraged not to open to their feelings because it is not consistent with our standard of masculinity. As a culture, we have done so well at teaching this to our boy children that we have successfully cut mature men off from their own feelings. Though we may feel the gross level of "good" or "bad," "up" and "down," for many men, the more subtle level of discernment necessary to get in touch with feelings and their truth is absent.

I worked with a client a number of years ago who was terribly dissatisfied with his work. In fact, he was also unhappy with his marriage and troubled about his relationship with his children. In short, his life was a torture. Yet when I would ask him how he felt he would say, "I *think* that . . . ." I would reply to these "I *think*" statements, "Let's leave your thoughts aside for the moment and concentrate on how you feel." Don would then reply, "Well, I *think* that . . ." This pattern was repeated over and over again, the entire time we worked together. He was never able to access his feelings, only the rational thinking function was available to him.

Don and I were unable to make any progress with the problems he faced at work. When he spoke of his family of origin, and his father, it was clear that he had learned to suppress his connection to his feelings as a child at home. Appearing not to feel was the thing for which he was rewarded with approval. Therefore, as a grown man, Don was not able to take the first step in his own healing, opening to the truth of his feelings. It wasn't anybody's "fault," he was a victim of social conditioning, just as his father had been before him.

The deep pain Don was suffering was cast in a cultural container as strong as cement. We could not crack the conditioned denial no matter how hard we tried. He could not even break through by smashing a tennis racquet against pillows to release his constricted anger. Don's was a case of the cruelty of our social conditioning. A case of how much pain the culture can inflict upon us, creating an almost impenetrable barrier between our awareness and the truth of our feelings.

Don came to his final session with me with his arm in a cast. He had fallen off a bicycle on a ride with his kids. I asked Don, "How do you feel about all this," and he said, "Well, I *think* that . . ."

The following exercise is an opportunity to discover and deepen the process of opening to the truth within us.

EXERCISE

An Experience With Self-Honesty

- Relax your body and quiet your mind.
- Bring to your attention an issue that is troubling you.
- Pay close attention to your thoughts, and notice the feelings in your body that are associated with them.
- Notice the movement of your thoughts, and the instances where the mind "skids off" a certain thought, and the feeling.
- Bring your attention back to that thought and its feeling, and stay with it in a state of close attention.
- Notice if there is an element of truth in this particular thought and feeling that you do not wish to acknowledge. (Perhaps this is

because it is in conflict with your values, or it seems unpleasant, or because you believe that if you really think or feel this way, it may require action that is distasteful or has problematic consequences.)

- Knowing that there is no need to take action on anything, allow yourself to open to the truth of this thought or feeling. If you begin to "skid off" again, gently bring yourself back.
- Now that you have opened to the truth, notice how you feel. Scan your body and see if it is more relaxed, more peaceful, and more powerful.

It is important to remember that you do not need to "do" something because you open to your truth. You are not forced into anything by knowing clearly what is true for you; your freedom of action and effectiveness is, in fact, greatly expanded because you have a more accurate understanding of "how it really is."

Truth-Telling To Others

Though truth-telling to ourselves is difficult, for many, it is even more difficult to speak our truth to others. To do so often feels dangerous. Underlying this feeling of danger is the fear of loss. We may feel that if we speak our truth to others, it will alienate or hurt them. Therefore we may lose their friendship and good will, or in the case of the workplace, our job or money.

This is entirely possible. Most of us know people who have lost their jobs because they spoke their truth. My friend worked with, and was in a relationship with, a man who was a batterer. When she felt empowered enough, she left him but continued in the same job. For three years she kept that secret, telling no one at work. Finally, when she could no longer stand the hypocrisy of his position of guidance and trust in the organization, she confronted him, "You either quit, or I tell the boss about your abusiveness." In the end, he did not quit and both of them were fired.

So, speaking the truth is not about doing the morally righteous thing for which we are always rewarded. In fact, the value of truth-telling is entirely apart from morality or outer reward. What we need to look at is what are the consequences to ourselves of withholding the truth, and what are the inner rewards for speaking it?

One of the major negative consequences of withholding our truth is the feeling of constriction and enslavement it produces. We don't want to share a truth because we fear the consequences. But the withholding often creates an even worse outcome, the strain of constriction.

It takes a substantial amount of energy to hold back an inner truth. This holding back creates stress. Withholding our truth is the psychic equivalent to the physical act of carrying weights around all day. It is a strain that can take a major toll.

Presently, stress in the workplace is a much discussed topic. Millions of dollars are spent every year to train corporate employees in stress reduction. My experience working with organizations is that the single biggest stress producing element in the workplace is withholding truth.

Of course, there may be a price to pay for speaking the truth at work. But, look at the price we pay for not speaking it: ulcers, headaches, back-pain, and low self-esteem. If we were to calculate in dollars and cents the loss to industry of our withholding, the figure would be astronomical.

Conversely, truth-telling is a liberating and energizing experience. One of the most powerful teachings of Jesus is, know your truth and speak your truth, for it is the "truth which shall set you free." Speaking the truth helps you feel good about yourself. Exactly because it is difficult and sometimes dangerous, truth-telling is empowering and builds self-confidence.

Truth-telling is the basis of authenticity. Those who speak the truth, even when it is not popular, are generally regarded as trustworthy by others. They hold a place of respect and honor in the workplace. Though they may make some enemies, and sometimes lose "goodies" in the short-term, truth-tellers are usually successful people.

Speaking truth is the basis for the development of trust between people at work. Trust is the cornerstone of good relations and the foundation for getting things done between people. When we trust each other, we can work successfully together.

Leadership in the workplace is the skill of getting the job done through people. The most important quality that facilitates successful leadership is trust between the leader and follower. Without trust, fear is the motivator. And fear as a motivator has severe limitations. It engenders a minimalist response from the follower and never calls forth excellence. Trust, on the other hand, motivates loyalty, creativity, and excellence.

So, it is extremely important for leaders to speak the truth, for bosses to be truthful with workers, and for co-workers to be truthful with each other. Through truth-telling, trust is built and the work gets done in ways that exceeds our expectations.

In the story of my friend who was fired because she spoke the truth of her abuse by her former partner, it would seem on first sight, that she lost from this experience. Yes, she lost her job, but she gained her freedom, self-respect, and confidence. She later moved into work that suited her far better and was much happier. "Overall," she told me, "I'm much better off for having released the secret, and getting fired, than holding that all inside, and keeping the job."

One of the reasons truth-telling is difficult for us is that most of us are conditioned to be "nice." We want others to think we are "nice" so they will "like" us. This is the foundation message many of us grew up with. Yet, this "niceness" is not kindness. It is not a deep caring or love for the other. "Nice" is for the most part, simply a way of being that does not offend. How different it is from true kindness, which is based upon truth. If we cannot speak our truth and be "nice," then "nice" is too shallow a quality to cultivate.

Another reason we find truth-telling difficult is that it may create conflict. If I speak my truth, and you don't like it, we have conflict. For many of us, avoiding conflict, like being "nice," has been a foundational message. They go together. As someone with a family history that said, "avoid interpersonal conflict at all cost," I can say, truth-telling and dealing with the conflict it may generate, is a healing and empowering experience. It is an antidote to the crippling effect of being fearful of conflict with others.

There is nothing wrong with conflict when it is necessary and appropriate. It can be enlivening and help us better understand who we are. Being "nice" and avoiding conflict are the cornerstones of our difficulties with truth-telling. It is a wonderful experience to declare our independence and release these constrictions. It is extremely enlivening to step into our maturity and stand in the clean fresh air of truth-telling.

Truth With Love

If we take as our standard, kindness, rather than niceness, then truth-telling with others, whether positive or critical, requires that we maintain a connection of the heart while sharing. That is, we speak truth with love. We maintain an awareness of the love connection between us and the other, even if we do not "like" the other, for love does not require liking.

Truth can be a vicious weapon. It can be an instrument of attack and harm. As most all of us have seen truth used as a weapon, we may have developed an attitude that it is better not to speak the truth because it causes pain. For the purposes of this discussion, let's distinguish between harm and pain. Pain is experienced in the moment and recedes quickly. Harm lingers.

Harm comes when the truth is spoken with the intent to hurt. If the intent is love, if the love connection is kept foremost in our consciousness while sharing our truth, even when it is critical, then short-term pain may result, but not long-term harm. It is rather like when we tell our children about their inoculation injections, "It will hurt for a second, but it will be good for you the rest of your life."

The encounter group movement of the1970s was based upon truth-telling. Unfortunately, the entire emphasis was on truth, the concern for love was absent. As a result, many people felt deeply wounded from these encounters; brutalized by another's truth. I have experienced this myself, a vicious verbal attack by someone in a group using their perception of me as the weapon. It was more than painful, it was harmful, leaving me wondering about myself and diminishing my confidence.

The "how to" of speaking truth with love is a simple but difficult process. That is, the process is not complex, but it requires courage and strength.

Bring to awareness your positive regard for the other. Actively hold that in your consciousness when you share your truth with them. If you do not like the other person, acknowledge that it is O.K. not to like them, and bring to mind their Essence. It is their personality we do not like, their Essence is of the same cloth as our own, a reflection of the universal Divine. Hold that Essence connection while sharing your truth, it may be painful to the other, but it will not cause harm.

This can be difficult because when anger wells up, we actually do want to harm the other. When we feel this, the skillful thing to do is to speak our feelings about ourselves as our truth, without blame, accusation, or attack. For instance, "I'm angry at you," or "I'm mad as hell," or something similar, focusing on the feelings we ourselves are experiencing, not our perception of them. This will help release and satisfy our anger. Later, when we are able to affirm the heart and Essence connection, we can share the truth of our perception with the other.

Will Schutz speaks of six levels of truth. The first, level zero, is when we are feeling something but don't express it. Level one is expressing the feelings, but blaming them on the other, like "You Jerk." Level two is focused on my feelings about you, "I dislike you." Level three adds insight by including why I dislike you. Level four further explains the process but level five is deepest form of truth telling. It arrives when we recognize how we feel about ourselves, withdraw our projections, and share our fears. Telling the truth about ourselves is for Schutz, the real truth-telling.[1]

Truth-Telling in Groups and Organizations

As we noted earlier, speaking the truth is the central vehicle for shifting a group or organization away from a dysfunctional pattern toward a healthy one. Truth is what is usually lacking in unhealthy groups, and dysfunctional patterns can be interrupted and broken with it. Truth-telling is a resource we all have and are capable of using. Therefore, we can all contribute to healing the groups and organizations we work in.

1. Will Schutz, *The Truth Option*, Ten Speed Press, Berkeley, 1984.

A powerful tool for facilitating truth-telling in the group setting is the Talking Staff. The Talking Staff is a gift of the Native American tradition. It is a wooden staff, adorned or plain, which the group agrees to endow symbolically with the power to help each speak truth from the heart.

The staff is passed around the group and each person drops deeper inside themselves, into their heart, and speaks the truth of their thoughts and feelings. While the person with the Staff speaks, the others remain silent and listen. It is a non-interactive, non-adversarial technique to bring truth forward.

One of the great merits of the Talking Staff is that it frees the listener from the need to construct a response. The effort to "figure out what we are going to say" interferes with our listening and ultimately distracts the speaker from going deeper.

Also, the speaker is relieved from having to "defend" his or her position. It is pure sharing, without the need to impose a false logic or construct an unassailable position. "Right" or "wrong," the feelings are simply true for the speaker. As a result, the atmosphere which the Talking Staff engenders in a group is profound and often very moving. It can shake a group out of its conspiracy of silence into a healthier, more dynamic organization.

A number of years ago, working with a law firm facilitating a team-building project, it became clear that the adversarial nature of their work had affected their office culture. They could not work cooperatively. They habitually disagreed and argued with each other, making the teamwork they desired impossible.

The Talking Staff was introduced at a weekend Retreat. I explained its meaning and how it was used. With the Staff in my hand to help me, I spoke the difficult truth I saw in their self-defeating culture.

After I finished, the Talking Staff lay untouched in the middle of the circle for ten long minutes. An eternity of silence. Finally, one attorney, the most intellectually oriented member of the staff, began to speak. His voice was significantly lower, quieter, and slower than I had ever heard it. He spoke of the pain of his isolation and the trap of always feeling compelled to listen for the flaws and holes in his colleagues' speech.

The long silence, followed by this deep, truthful sharing had a powerful impact. It unlocked the whole organization from its dysfunctional pattern. One after another, each attorney spoke their truth and pain. It was clear that everyone longed to work together cooperatively but felt stuck in a competitive mode.

This experience was the beginning of a dramatic shift in the direction, culture, and structure of the entire organization, which three years of previous consulting work had not been able to accomplish. Six years later, the organization is still growing and healthy.

"Keeping current" with our communication regarding our feelings about others is important. A major cause of problems between people is the buildup of unexpressed feelings. Resentment is the state we experience when we hold in our negative feelings. If someone does or says something we don't like, and we remain silent, the negative energy turns inward. We can cause ourselves and others a good deal of harm through this repression and suppression. Resentment is one of the most insidious of emotions. It feels awful inside, does a great deal of mental, emotional, and physical harm, and it pollutes the atmosphere of a group.

Often, when I am called into an organization, no matter what the outer symptoms, the underlying issue is unspoken feelings that have built up a wall of resentment. Though the problem may be experienced by the organization as "production has dropped" or "the managers need more training," or "there is conflict between Marketing and Sales," what I actually find is a mountain of "unfinished interpersonal business." That is, a history of mutual hurts between people that have never been directly and truthfully confronted, leaving the atmosphere heavy-laden with resentment. In such an atmosphere, a business cannot flourish. It is understandable that production drops, or profits take a downward turn, or managers can no longer lead.

In the business world, particularly, there is a great fear of truth-telling. People are afraid of its impact on peoples' feelings and its negative effect on organizational effectiveness. In fact, the exact opposite is more often true. Not sharing the truth of our feelings in the business setting, and the resentment it engenders, is one of the most significant causes of our present state of organizational ineffectiveness and international competitive disadvantage.

In a culture like ours, if we are to be effective in business, we must release the creativity of the worker. Now, it is constricted in a mountain of resentment, not speaking our feelings and resenting the relationships we have with our bosses and co-workers. As a result we are mediocre.

When I enter an organization, besides addressing the reported symptoms, I always look for opportunities to support people in sharing their accumulated unspoken truth. This process of "getting current" is ultimately the most important element in personal and group healing as well as the key to improving organizational effectiveness.

The Gestalt perspective in psychology asserts that "unfinished business" is the major barrier to psychological well being. When we are burdened and constricted with unresolved energy, we can not perform effectively, there is not sufficient energy to act competently in the present. When we "take care of old business," that is speak our truth to others, then we have sufficient natural vitality to creatively deal with all that challenges us in the present. From the Gestalt perspective, psychological health and personal effectiveness are not overly complex matters. If we keep current within ourselves and with others, the life-force we naturally have is sufficient to successfully face and solve the problems presented by everyday life.

Recently I was facilitating a discussion for a client group, a physician's office, in which one of the nurses said she had a problem with the way the doctor had greeted a patient yesterday. He didn't pay enough attention to the patient, she said, and it seemed disrespectful. She went on to say that it particularly "pushed her buttons" because the doctor had been very strident with her, "lectured me a lot," she said, "about how this is a 'patient centered' practice. The patient is supposed to be King around here, and you treated her like junk."

When I asked Bill, the doctor if he had a response to this, he said, "I don't think I have anything to say right now." He was fidgeting, and twisting in the chair, obviously angry and withdrawn. As I encouraged him to speak his feelings, he said, "I know Dorothy is right about that incident yesterday, but there seems like there is something else going on here. I'm feeling too bad for this to just be a problem of my poor greeting to a patient on a busy day."

As we explored further, Bill said, "It is as if there is a lot of other garbage coming at me along with this criticism. I don't mind hearing that I made a mistake, but the way she's talking, it seems like I'm an awful S.O.B. for doing it."

As we worked with this material further, it eventually became apparent that Dorothy was holding a lot of resentment toward the doctor that she had not expressed. And, the negative feelings were all coming out around this one incident. The mistake Bill had made was not terribly important, but Dorothy's unspoken and unresolved resentment was.

With time and truth-telling, they sorted it out. They went over the accumulated material that was beneath this issue and found that Bill had been frustrated in his efforts to develop a closer working relationship with Dorothy. He had been close with his previous assistant and now felt the loss.

Dorothy, on the other hand, experienced Bill's overtures of friendship as threatening. It scared her coming from a man in a position of authority, her boss. Each time Bill moved toward her in a gesture of friendship, she moved away.

The underlying dynamic generating this interpersonal and organizational problem was not the way the doctor greeted patients, it was the desire for greater intimacy by one party and the fear of it by another. The real issue, however, was not the difference in feelings or needs for intimacy, it was that the differences and discomforts went unspoken. Dorothy was too afraid to speak and Bill was too embarrassed. Once the truth-telling was done, the feelings and perspectives shared, the air was clear, old business became current, and the friendship began to grow.

The following exercise is a way to practice your truth-telling to others. It will give you the experience of speaking appreciations you may never have shared, and cleaning up unfinished business with a friend. This exercise will deepen and strengthen your relationship with your exercise partner.

"Sharing Appreciations and Withholds"

- Choose a friend with whom you feel comfortable and safe.
- Ask if they will agree to do an exercise with you in which you share the things you like about each other and the things you have problems with in the other.
- Sit across from each other, in a comfortable position, and look each other in the eye. Keep the eye contact the entire time you are doing the exercise.(Maintaining direct eye contact in our culture is challenging, but if you can do it, you will be well rewarded.)
- To begin, share with your friend what it is you appreciate about them. Take your time, allow pauses, wait and see if more comes, stay with it until your are relatively certain you're done. When you have finished sharing all the ways in which you appreciate your friend, switch roles.
- Your friend now speaks their appreciations to you.
- When your partner is complete, it's time to deal with the more difficult side of the unspoken material. Share with your friend the things about them that have been a problem for you, or which you dislike but have been afraid to speak and have been withholding until now.
- While sharing this material, remember to maintain a "heart connection." Before beginning, silently reaffirm within you the love you have for your friend, and in this context share the withholds.
- When you are finished, ask the other person to share their withholds with you. Remind them to first reaffirm their heart connection, and then proceed. When you are complete, maintain the eye contact for a short time and acknowledge the difficult and worthwhile work you have done together.
- Notice how you feel after completing this work. See if there is more openness and freedom within in you, and between you and your partner.
- Watch the relationship over the coming weeks and months, and notice if it deepens, becoming even more satisfying and rewarding than it was before.
- Imagine what it would be like to do this with all the people you are close with. Imagine what it would be like to do this exercise with your colleagues at work.

6 ❧ On Taking Responsibility for Ourselves

To become one's self is man's true vocation.
KIERKEGARD

Though the social and economic context plays an important role in shaping our lives, if we wish to gain control over our work, we must acknowledge and own our part in creating it. By taking personal responsibility for our role in creating our work, we are empowered to construct an alternative that is more satisfying.

It is common to blame others for our problems. Though sometimes our distress is the direct result of another's behavior, or our place in the social economic order, most of our dissatisfaction is self-induced. It is the result of our thoughts, feelings, and behavior. We are most often the authors of our own pain.

Though we are in the habit of thinking, "It's my wife's fault that I'm unhappy, or it's my students' fault that I'm having problems, or it's my friends' fault that I feel uncomfortable," the truth is, it's usually my "fault," if there is any fault at all. The problem with blaming others is that it is disempowering. If the situation I am in is someone else's fault, then someone else has created it, and someone else is in control of my life. I am powerless to change my life. By blaming others for our problems at work, we make ourselves victims.

Ultimately, the only person I have the power to change is myself. If I own my feelings, that is, if I take responsibility for creating them, then I am able to change. This is one of the most empowering shifts we can experience, from an attitude of "I can't," to an attitude of "I can."

The most significant barrier to our taking responsibility for ourselves is that it feels good to blame someone else for our troubles. Through blaming others, in the short run, we escape feeling the blame ourselves. Many of us learned this pattern in childhood, as an effective way to avoid punishment. Its long term consequence, in adult life, however, is self-victimization.

The way out is to understand and skillfully work with the psychological process called "projection." Negative projection is an unconscious process that functions to defend ourselves from psychic discomfort. Through projection, we avoid the dissatisfaction we have with ourselves, by casting it onto others. Instead of seeing and feeling the aspects of ourselves that are confused, unresolved or which we dislike, and experiencing the discomfort, we project those qualities onto the people around us.

The other face of this phenomena is called positive projection. Through it, we project onto others the positive parts of ourselves that we are not willing to own. Sometimes we are not willing to take on the responsibility of being kind, or beautiful, or intelligent. For instance, I may see my boss as all powerful and all knowing, a superman. In this case, it is likely that I am projecting my power and wisdom, that I am unable or unwilling to own, onto my boss.

Because projection occurs below the conscious level, we are not aware of it. People become defensive and angry when they are told that their blaming is projection. At the conscious level, they believe the situation really is the fault of someone else.

One of the great values in learning to see through our projections is that it provides us a window into our unconscious. Understanding our projections and taking responsibility for our feelings is a way to bring to consciousness that which has previously been unconscious. As Carl Jung said, in speaking of the unexamined projection process, "Projection makes the whole world a replica of our unknown face."

When we feel blame arising, it is most skillful to assume that a projection is emerging; an unconscious aspect of ourselves is coming to the surface. It is an opportunity for rewarding self-examination and introspection. We can discover our hidden selves and release the blocks and barriers to fully satisfying work.

Noticing the projection process in ourselves, taking responsibility for our feeling, and "withdrawing" our projections is a healing and growth-producing effort. Withdrawing projections means to take back to ourselves the qualities we have cast out onto others. Realizing that my anger with you is really my anger with myself is withdrawing the projection.

To be aware that we are projecting and then to withdraw projections has far reaching implications for ourselves and others. Until we are able to take responsibility for our internal darkness, there will be no true peace; not in our lives, our families, our work, our communities, the nation, or the world. Violence must be addressed and pacified at its source. If we try to make peace on the outside while there is war on the inside, it will not succeed.

I went to an International Conference on Peace recently where one hundred and fifty people from all around the world gathered to promote peace. In fact, the conference was one of the most emotionally violent gatherings I have ever attended. Few of the participants were willing to acknowledge and address their own inner conflicts. All the effort was devoted to asking others — politicians, corporations, and the military — to stop their violence. Massive social processes and structures were designed to bring peace to the world, while people were mean, short tempered, and sometime ruthless with each other.

I believe that from a violent seed the flower of peace cannot bloom. Because of our lack of skillfulness and unwillingness to look inside for the real sources of violence, this group only succeeded in adding more hurt, division, and disharmony to a world desperately in need of peace.

The conference was a large-scale example of people unwilling to deal with their projections, and the difficulty and harm that results. It was a great lesson for me in not trying to make something happen on the outside until I am working with it on the inside.

The following exercise is designed to help you become aware of the projection process, begin to withdraw blame, and learn to use the projection process as a rich resource for personal and vocational growth.

EXERCISE

Working With Projections: Who At Work is Upsetting You?

- Close yours eyes and relax. Put your attention on your breath. Allow any tension to be released in your exhaling breath. Feel yourself getting fully relaxed from toes to head.
- Bring to mind someone in your work life who is upsetting you. Bring their face into clear view.
- Look at them, without emotion, and notice what characteristics they have that are upsetting you.
- Let their face recede and bring your attention back to the breath. Notice it as it goes in and out. Exhale any tension that may have been built up on the exhaling breath.
- Still with your eyes closed, very lightly and experimentally, notice if any of the qualities you found in the person upsetting you are qualities you have in yourself that are unresolved or which you don't like.
- Now, see if there is someone else in you work life that is upsetting you. Go through this same process with them. Continue this process, one by one, with all the people in your work life who are upsetting you, until you are complete.
- Notice if over the coming days and weeks, you feel more insight into yourself, and less anger with co-workers, subordinates, and bosses.

It is useful to develop a refined sense of when a feeling is the result of a projection or when it is a "clear" response to another. A clear response is a feeling that is accurate, it is not coming from another source of which you are unaware. It is an authentic feeling about the other, as opposed to a projection onto the other of feelings about yourself. If your feelings are a clear response to another, you will not be able to trace the feelings back to inner dissatisfaction or confusion. The way to make this discernment is to use the process for gaining insight into feelings described in Chapter Four.

For example, I was recently in Maui, Hawaii. For the first few days, thoughts like "There are too many people here, too many tourists, too much traffic" rambled through my head. At the same time, I felt a strong sense of missing my daughter, who was still in California. Both sentiments were disturbing.

When I sat quietly with them, I came to understand that my dissatisfaction with Maui was really "homesickness." I was projecting my dissatisfaction with being away from home onto this place. There is nothing wrong on Maui, there was something wrong inside Howie.

Conversely, when I sat with the feeling of missing my daughter, nothing else came up. There was nothing beneath that feeling. I love her, I miss her, and I was sad. That was that. It was a clear feeling, not a projection.

Looking back, the two feeling states were quite different. The dissatisfaction with place had a "tinny" quality. It was wholly mental, not a deep emotion. I was critical, I had lots of judgments, I had lots of ideas and reasons about what was wrong. The quality of missing my daughter was more profound, deeper, not a critical response, but an authentic sadness.

When we sense we are holding negative feelings about someone at work, before focusing all our attention on the other and how to change them, the best strategy is to take responsibility for our feelings. Stay with them until insight arises about their source. If the feeling is clear, either no information will arise, or the information that comes up will confirm the clear response. If it is a projection, information will come forward about the true source of the feeling within yourself.

The key to using this process to your advantage is slowing down. Before you act out your feelings on another, go inside, see what is really true. Remember, in doing this, allow the thinking process to be at rest, and see if there is some sensation in your body associated with the feelings you are experiencing. Notice if there is one area in your body that is feeling the strongest sensation. Put all of your attention there. Stay with that sensation and allow information to "bubble up" from that place.

Perhaps you are angry at a colleague for being sloppy in her work. When you sit with the anger notice where it is lodged in your body and listen to your body for information. It may turn out that you are not satisfied with the quality of your own work, and that is what really needs the attention.

On the other hand, you may find that your feelings are not a projection, and that the most appropriate behavior is to make an effort to influence her to improve the quality of her work. Selecting the appropriate behavior, as a result of knowing how to dance with projections and feelings, will allow you to be much more effective and satisfied at work.

The Cycle of Blame and Defense

Over the years, working with groups and organization, I have found that "disowned" projections are at the root of many interpersonal problems. I call this the cycle of blame and defense. It is a pattern of interaction in which one person projects blame unto another. The blamed person then reacts by defending himself and in turn also projects blame. The interaction enters a downward spiral, in which each party continues to blame the other and defend himself. A positive outcome seldom results from this cycle.

Because blaming is avoiding the responsibility for one's own part in a problem, it puts the interaction on a false footing. The actual problem, created by all the parties involved, cannot be resolved until the participants take responsibility. It's like trying to treat an arm pain that originates in the heart and lungs by soaking the arm. Cure is not effective unless it addresses all the sources involved in creating the disease.

Further, because in this cycle both parties feel blamed, they react defensively and are unable to engage in a cooperative solution.

For example, the fragile goods of a glassware company were arriving damaged to retailers at a higher rate than normal. The quality control manager, unconscious of her feelings of guilt for allowing the condition to exist, went to the shipping foreman and launched into a tirade of blame. The shipping foreman reacted in defense and anger and projected his unconscious guilt by blaming her for not doing her job. Now, we have a typical work place mess. A problem is deepening and interpersonal conflict is growing. This is the cycle of blame and defense.

Alternatively, if upon hearing of the high rate of damaged goods, the quality control manager had taken responsibility for her feelings, opened to them, and stayed with them until she understood their meaning, she could have gone to the shipping manger in a "clear" state and asked him to work with her to solve the problem. He, under those conditions, would most likely have welcomed the opportunity to cooperatively solve the problem and recognized his own part in creating it.

The alternative to the cycle of blame and defense is the process of identifying needs and meeting them. For example, a supervisor and a statistician working for a life insurance company are in disagreement about the accuracy of the latest actuarial data their department has generated. The supervisor senses the desire to blame her employee arising within her. Instead of blaming, however, she owns her feelings and enters into a self-examination process. She stays with the feeling and soon understands that the anger is really with herself for not providing sufficient supervision. Now, in a clear state, with no need to blame or defend, she is free to discover what is going on below the surface for the statistician. Asking a few questions, she discovers that what he really needs, underneath his blaming of her, is assistance with his work. The new formulae for producing the actuarial figures are going over his head, he is frustrated and scared. At this point, the supervisor is able to sit with her employee and provide the technical help that both reassures him and results in the production of accurate data.

Another example of the alternative to the cycle of blame and defense, identifying needs and meeting them, can be seen in the experience of a small moving company. An executive in the company was furious with his secretary because she made too many mistakes in typing his letters. This continued after numerous conversations about the subject. As he began to blame her once again, he slowed down and sensed the feeling tone in his body. He noticed a discomfort in his throat and remained with the feeling. Soon, it came to him that he was not satisfied with his own level of communication. He just could not seem to find the right words to express himself in speech or writing. He realized that what he was really unhappy with was his letters, the secretary's errors were just "pushing that button."

Once this was understood, he was able to talk to his secretary with a clear mind and heart. "Jean, what's going on? We've discussed these typing errors three times and they keep coming up. What can we do about it? Is there any way I can help?"

"Well," she said, "actually I hate making mistakes worse than you hate seeing them. But the truth is, they aren't typing errors, they're spelling errors. I don't know how to spell well enough, and I've always been too embarrassed about it to say anything. It makes me feel stupid. What would really help me is a spell-checking program for the computer. I'm sure with that, I could learn to clear up most of the problems."

The boss, of course, was delighted. With a modest investment in software, the problem was solved. By taking responsibility for his own feelings, identifying the needs of his secretary and meeting them, the moving company executive was able to break the cycle of blame and defense and generate a constructive, effective solution.

Bosses

Being a boss and relating to our bosses are challenging parts of work life. Bosses are generally the most powerful authority figures in our adult lives. Most of us have unresolved feelings about authority as a result of prolonged subservience to parents and teachers during our childhood years.

We have personal histories that include years of domination by adults. Can you remember that feeling of impotence, as a child, when you really wanted to do something and you could not simply because a parent said, "No"? When we were children, the adults had most of the power, we had little. Whether our parents and teachers were fair or not, whether they loved us or not, whether it was "for our own good" or not, that frustration of our strong, natural desires, produces powerful, often lingering, resentment toward people in positions of authority.

Because many of us are not clear of these resentments, feelings about people in authority remain a difficult issue in our lives. Relating to the most dominant authority figures in our adult lives, our bosses, is often a confused and perplexing matter. Working under a boss, or being a boss, is very challenging because, through this relationship, we are unconsciously trying to resolve and heal a lifetime of unfinished business with authority. These conditions are a greenhouse for projections.

My experience observing people in positions of leadership in business is that bosses are magnets for negative authority projections. The egalitarian and democratic ethic in our society reinforces our negative projections and supports our natural tendency to blame those in power for our work problems. In the case of bosses, our projections carry the added intensity of righteousness. We often feel we hold the democratic moral high ground, knowing with religious certainty that we are right and that "they" are to blame for my problems.

I, too, am a child of our egalitatrian and democratic ethos and have unresolved authority issues as well. As a consultant to organizations, however, I have had the opportunity to watch the dynamic of "leader bashing" as an objective observer. It is clear, that in many cases, bosses draw far more criticism than they deserve and are blamed for far more problems than they create.

Most of us are unconscious of our authority projections. We have no idea that our displeasure, blame, or hatred of the boss may be "our own stuff" thrown onto "them." Usually we are certain how wrong "they" are, and how right "we" are. As certain as when we cried out to our parents, in total frustration, "I hate you!"

Lately, there has been a rash of presidential firings at universities with which I have been associated. Some have been in the most gruesome and cruel manner. At one university, the president, who whatever his failings, was a dedicated sincere hard working leader, was informed that he must come home immediately from his sabbatical in India, because the Board of Trustees was considering revoking his contract. He did, and they fired him.

I see these firings, because of their insensitivity and cruelty, as the result of unresolved hatred of authority; the collective projections of those doing the firing. Though I know they are unaware of it and would vehemently deny it, I see their action as personal historical material manifested in these acts of retribution. We project our hatred and act on it. We project our sense of helplessness in the face of authority, and when we have a chance we "kill the leader."

This is true of political leaders as well. Aside from the issues of how well they represent us, how responsible, wise, or humane they are, political leaders are flak catchers for our resentment of authority. There they stand, publicly, in the newspapers and on T.V., with all their power lorded over us. It pushes our authority buttons, and we lash out with anger and blame.

Sometimes, our positive authority projections are cast upon our bosses and political leaders as well. Occasionally there comes a leader whom we see as "the greatest;" the most caring, sensitive, intelligent, capable individual we know. We turn this person into a hero, as we did in the early 1960s with John Fitzgerald Kennedy. Heroes, of course, are the recipients of our collective positive projections. As we did to JFK, we annoint such heroes as the embodiment of the kind of authority we wish our parents would have been, or our teachers would have been, or our bosses would be. The kind of authority we wish we could be.

When we are in the boss or leadership position ourselves, the projection phenomena is maddening. I was facilitating a group meeting as part of an organization development program with a business recently, and a discussion about the dissatisfaction with a boss emerged. We talked about it in rational terms for a while, and then things turned more emotional and heated. Accusations started flying, the cycle of blame and defense kicked in full force.

Suddenly, the boss, Art, spoke out, "Wait a minute," he shouted, "what the hell is this? It happens over and over again. I do something and all of a sudden everybody else knows why I did it, and what it really means, and a whole bunch of other things. People don't ask me, or check with me about their interpretations. They just know they're right and I'm wrong. I'm the one to blame. Later, I hear through the grapevine what a jerk I was. You people have no idea what I'm doing or why I'm doing it. This stuff you're talking about is a bunch of baloney."

Art's anger turned to frustration. Whatever his shortcomings around communication were, he was obviously very moved, frustrated, and saddened at being constantly misinterpreted and misunderstood. Later, he said, " This whole thing makes me feel helpless and angry."

Because Art had the courage to speak the truth of his feelings, this meeting helped the organization and the employees move through some of their problems. It gave everyone a "blood and guts" sense of what it feels like to be on the receiving end of collective projections. It gave us all an opportunity to discuss the phenomena of unexamined projections, and the way they act as a barrier to satisfying work.

It is a challenge to have a clear relationship with your bosses. To see them for who they really are, not what we project upon them. Projecting our resentment of authority onto our leaders interferes with our ability to engage in rewarding work on a day to day basis. Unexamined authority projections keep us locked in emotional reactions, which are not authentic responses that help us grow, but diversions on a road to nowhere.

Skillfully dealing with authority projections is one of the most constructive things you can do to Rekindle the Spirit in Work. When you feel reactive to your boss, go inside yourself. Notice if some of your reaction is unresolved feelings, stemming from your personal history. Sit quietly with those feelings. Feel deeply, and allow insight and information to come up that will help release you from the constriction of this reactivity.

Relations With Co-Workers

Sometimes at work we have the experience of feeling verbally abused or attacked, not by our bosses, but by our co-workers. Doing interpersonal battle on the job is not pleasant. It is a significant impediment to satisfying work.

There is no easy solution to this problem. We can recognize, however, that when co-workers are attacking and abusive, it is likely that their projections have been activated. They are throwing onto you their dissatisfaction with themselves.

Their responses are out of proportion to the situation because their reaction is not rooted in the situation. Its source resides in festering material inside themselves. The truth is, most people at work don't care enough about us to get as excited as they do when they are abusive. They care very much, however, about themselves.

All that anger or blame is really frustration at not being who they would like to be.

Knowing this does not stop their attack, but it gives us some perspective and the good sense to remain outside their projection system. It is not helpful in the emotionally charged moment to ask them to take responsibility for their own feelings. That will make them more angry, as they are unaware that they are projecting and want their blaming to be taken seriously.

The key for us, however, is not to get caught in the web of our co-workers' unresolved psychological material. To know that their attack is a projection, not a clear response and that it comes out of their personal history allows us to temper our response. We don't have to get "sucked in," believing their blame is authentic. Don't be drawn in at the level at which the blame is presented. Don't respond to the accusations; it can never pacify the real source of their dissatisfaction, self-anger.

If someone at work gets very angry with you because you don't keep your desk tidy, you can allow yourself to be drawn in to that fight and argue about your right to have your desk as you want it, or you can try to please them and tidy it. Neither response is likely to satisfy the complainer. Your neatness is not his real concern, it is his own neatness, or lack of it, that is bothering him. Most likely, he has uncomfortable feelings about orderliness. Perhaps he took abuse in his childhood, or the military about personal neatness. Or perhaps he has tendency to be sloppy, but works very hard to counteract it and is extremely orderly. Whatever the reason, any co-worker coming on strong about our neatness is likely to be dealing with their own issues on the subject.

On the other hand, someone who is naturally neat and keeps their life in order with ease is likely not to care about the tidiness of your desk. Because they are clear about the issue, they have no charge about it, and no need for you to change in order to satisfy them.

Don't get drawn into endless and frustrating interactions with co-workers about what you are doing wrong, know that it is likely to be a projection on their part. Don't try to solve the problem at the level they present it or allow yourself to be abused because of their unwillingness to take responsibility for their own feelings.

Conclusion

Though it is often true that problems in the workplace are the result of social and economic factors, structural issues, and unequal distribution of power, what we have most immediate control over is ourselves. If we learn to identify our projections, understand their messages, and withdraw them from our co-workers, bosses, and subordinates, we can make our work life infinitely more satisfying and rewarding. If we shift our framework and see projections as a gift, we can go even farther.

Projections are the messengers of the unconscious. They bring to light the well springs of our actions that are hidden in the darkness. When we are driven by internal forces that we cannot see, we are slaves to that darkness. Projections can be one of our greatest teachers. Through them we can learn what we need to know to take the next step in growing our work.

Some time ago, my partner Barbara and I sensed some deadness and antipathy in our relationship. We talked about not living together, having separate places, or getting a studio for more alone time. Though there was nothing intrinsically "wrong" with these thoughts or reactions, they did not get to the heart of the matter.

We left things alone for a while and then had another talk. I'm not sure where it began or what we talked about at first, but we were creating a positive context for going deeper together by avoiding blame and criticism.

All of a sudden, rage came up in me. "I'm enormously pissed about this feminist stuff you've been into for the last year. It feels angry and mean, and I feel like you make me personally responsible for the oppression of the system."

I recalled all the hurt I had felt around Barbara's growing strident feminism. How, though speaking out sometimes, I mostly held the anger silently. I sat there and allowed myself to fully open to the rage I had not been willing to feel. The inside of my mouth felt like it was on fire, like a volcano about to erupt.

I realized I was feeling the sensations in my body I had felt as a child. The same constriction, suppression, and imprisonment I had felt then when I wasn't allowed to speak out in anger.

In that moment it became clear that I was projecting old self-repression and constriction onto Barbara. Through the process of feeling the feelings and taking responsibility for ourselves, we cleared the dispute and its associated bad feelings and gained a new sense of internal freedom while at the same time deepening and strenghtening our relationship.

When we penetrated the projection through self-examination and discussion, we were released. We were empowered and able to be more of who we are in relationship and work.

7 SIGNS & SYMBOLS IN DAILY LIFE INFORMATION FOR ACTION

Are you looking for me? I am in the next seat.
My shoulder is against yours,
You will not find me in stupas, not in Indian shrine rooms,
nor in synagogues, nor in cathedrals:
not in masses, nor kirtans, not in legs winding
around your own neck, nor eating nothing but vegetables.
When you really look for me, you will see me instantly —
you will find me in the tiniest house of time.
Kabir says: Student, tell me, what is God?
He is the breath inside the breath.

KABIR

There is a rich source of guidance available to us in the symbolism of everyday life. The symbolic meaning of events that appear in the course of our lives can help us better understand ourselves and serve as signs pointing in the direction of satisfying work.

To understand the signs and symbols of daily life and use them for guidance, we need to extend our comprehension beyond the literal, to see events and experiences as having multiple levels of meaning. When I am thinking about my work and my back begins to hurt, at one level, my back simply hurts. At another level, a symbolic event has occurred from which I can gain insight into my work.

Sometimes the symbolic meaning of an event can be understood as a sign, providing direction for action. My back pain may be a sign that I am "carrying too much weight" in my work and indicate a need to let go of some of the responsibility I feel.

In this chapter we will discuss the symbolic meaning of messages from the body, information contained in the unexpected or accidental occurrences of daily life, and the guidance contained in dreams. We will also discuss the insight and direction that can be gained through intentionally using a symbol system, or oracle, such as the *I-Ching*, the *Tarot*, and the *Rekindling the Spirit in Work* cards.

Sigmund Freud believed that everything that happens in our lives is meaningful. Carl Jung believed that everything in life can be understood as symbolic. Taken together, these assumptions are the basis of understanding the signs and symbols of daily life. Everything that happens in our lives, both the sublime and the mundane, can be seen as more than a simple occurrence, they are footprints of our identity, and road maps for our direction.

When we speak of symbolism, we mean understanding a thing at a deeper level of significance. For example, the cross is a simple image consisting of one vertical line crossed by one horizontal line. Yet this plain object holds enormous symbolic meaning; the life of the Prophet Jesus of Nazarus, the death of the Lord Jesus the Christ, the Gospels, Christ's teachings, love, forgiveness, the Catholic church, the Protestant church, the Greek Orthodox church, the clergy, and so on.

We can think of many things in this way. The ocean is a body of water. It also can be a symbol of power, love, and beauty. Fire is heat and can be a symbol of inspiration and creativity. Earth is the planet we walk on and can be the symbol of stability and structure.

Symbols, for our purposes, should not be understood as having fixed meanings that apply to all people for all time. Symbols are personal. The cross has a different meaning for a Catholic, a Jew, a Hindu, or a Native American. The immense value of symbols is that they serve as a screen upon which the content of our personal unconscious can be projected into our awareness, and understood.

One of the reasons so few people look to the guidance of symbolism in their lives is the commonly held belief that there are universal standard meanings for symbols that we must know if we want to make sense of them. Quite the opposite is true. The symbols in our daily life are personal and individual. They grow out of our own unique psychological history.

We can treat our experiences, at one level, like a Rorschach test; the process whereby we read stories into images formed by ink blots on paper. Everyone sees the images differently and interprets the symbols uniquely, though the actual image on the blotter is the same.

You see one thing, I see another, everyone sees him or herself in the blots.

The symbols emerging from our bodies, events in our lives, and dreams can be treated like the Rorschach. They provide a screen that allows our interior movie to be shown in the theatre of the conscious.

It is important to know that to use the symbols that appear in our lives as signs and guidance, one need not be formally trained in symbology. There is no need for prior education to begin working with symbols to open to the information they provide.

When I look out the window of my office and I see a rabbit in the field across the way, at one level I have simply seen a rabbit. If I wish, however, I can play with the symbolic meaning. And, I do not need to know the ancient Chinese, Greek, or Roman meaning of the rabbit symbol. All I need do is slip past the rational and censoring mind and let loose my association with the animal image of rabbit. For me it is timid, timidity. Now, how does that apply to my work? Am I being too timid? Do I need to be more timid? What about timidity in work do I need to look at more closely?

The symbolic helps us to loosen the stranglehold of reason. It gives us access to information that is otherwise censored and locked away. As a result of our socialization, we have strong censoring processes based on morality and fear. Thoughts and feelings that conflict with our moral code or feel dangerous are not allowed into consciousness. Because of this, we are operating with partial information about ourselves, creating discomfort and confusion, and weakening our ability to make decisions in our overall best interest.

The various parts of ourselves that are suppressed in the unconscious, however, will not be denied. They will press outwards until they are acknowledged. They will cause confusion, pain, even accidents and physical illness, until they are recognized. The symbolic realm, if we allow it, can act as a translator for this information to pass from the realm of the hidden to the realm of the known.

The vehicle for this transformation is the projective process. Through it, we cast onto the symbol the meaning we have inside. We can allow ourselves to attribute meaning to symbols through the method of free association.

When I feel a throbbing between my shoulders, I slow down and put my attention there. The image that freely comes to me is a blade. A medieval hatchet, in the form of two crescents. I stay with that image and ask "What do you represent?" and it says, "Being stabbed in the back." I say, "Tell me more," and the blade says, "You feel stabbed in the back by your co-workers. They are letting you and the whole organization down with their petty turf interests."

Before I experienced the pain between my shoulders, I wasn't willing to let that knowledge in. I liked these people and would not allow into my mind the feeling of their betrayal. Now that I was clear, my actions could be more skillful and effective with my co-workers, and the awareness itself released me from the physical pain.

There is no need to assume any guiding hand is directing symbols to appear as the proper signs for guidance in our lives. This is a process that happens because the knowledge within us is emerging for self-direction and will use the symbolic level to communicate with the conscious mind.

I sometimes play with a 78 card deck of symbols known as the Tarot. The deck I use was created by James Wanless and is called the Voyager Tarot. The visual images on the cards, the symbols, are contemporary, using collage as the medium. Each card also has a descriptive word on it, such as Brilliance, Compassion, Disappointment, and so on. These cards, with their diverse visual images and words, serve as a wonderful screen upon which we can project what is going on inside us. We can select a card with the intention of getting direction about work. If we bypass the censor, we can look at the card and release our hidden inner knowledge, by projecting it onto the symbols.

I draw a card now that says "Master," and has the image of an old woman on it, weaving a basket. For me, as I look at this card, I associate it with wisdom, skill, and the satisfaction that comes with maturity. Also, I see mother and female power. I see the guidance of this symbolism for me in my work. I wish to achieve mastery, to have the skill and wisdom in all that I do that this old woman has in her weaving. I am willing to put in the time and effort to achieve it.

I had a client in a Rekindling the Spirit workshop who had recently been fired from his job. It was a very painful experience, as he had been the Executive Director of a social service agency that he helped build from a small organization on the edge of financial ruin to one of the largest, healthiest, not-for-profit agencies in the San Francisco Bay Area. He went through a bitter battle for months with the Board of Directors over differences in administrative philosophy. Eventually he lost and was fired.

During an exercise in the workshop, Blaine was the first to select a Tarot card. When he looked at it he said, "Oh my God, this fits perfectly. This is just what I have been experiencing. It says, Torture. I have been through torture in this process and now it's over. It's time for me to rest and lick my wounds. I need to let go of the fight." Up to that moment, he had continued to struggle with how wrong the Board had been, and what he could do about it. Now, he completely let go and relaxed. His face and body transformed. He looked like he had just dropped an enormous load.

At the same time, I thought, "There is nothing in the deck with the word Torture on it." Sitting next to him, I leaned over and looked at his card. I read it and pointed out to him that the word written on the bottom was not Torture, but Fortune. We laughed. Even a written word, so specific in form, had to move aside and act as a symbol because of Blaine's powerful inner need to recognize the effect on him of the firing, and to know that it was now time to rest and heal.

The Symbolism of the Body

Our bodies bring us a wealth of information in symbolic form. The process of accessing information from our feelings by focusing on the felt sense in the body has been discussed in depth. We can employ the same method with the physical sensations arising directly out of pain or illness.

For example, I was working yesterday, and during a break, I began to feel pain in my teeth. As I focused my attention, I got a sense that the discomfort I was feeling was from too much pressure. It felt like I was grinding.

The symbolism, for me, was obvious. I was pushing too hard in my writing. I was grinding it out, instead of letting it flow, and the body is letting me know, through the teeth. At the moment I had that insight, I experienced a deep breath and a sense of understanding. The discomfort in the teeth began to subside.

It wasn't an organic problem in my teeth, the result of injury, decay, or disease. It was the body using metaphor to bring me information. I was so intent on finishing the chapter that day, I was not paying attention to my overall well being. So, the body brought forward the pain, as a message; "pay attention!"

Unfortunately, most of us do not realize that feelings coming from the body can also be understood at the symbolic level. If we do not heed the initial signals, the body may continue to send us messages, even increase the level of the pain, until we "get it."

My experience is that even organic disease, or injury, usually also contains symbolic meaning. I spoke of a client earlier who was out of touch with his feelings. At the beginning of the last session, Bob came in with a cast, he had broken his right arm. The content of what Bob had been working on was his inability to get the job he wanted, and sort things out with his wife and children. The broken right arm, besides being the obvious result of an accident, also represented symbolically that inability to get things done in the world.

I spoke of the woman in my seminar who felt strong pain in her pelvis. When she worked with the pain, in symbolic terms, as a metaphor for something deeper, a great anger emerged. She felt unfulfilled sexually in her relationship with her husband. Upon understanding the meaning of the constriction in the pelvis, the pain began to subside and eventually went away.

Common illnesses, such as the flu or a cold, are often signals to slow down. We go at such a fast pace in our work, we often override the subtle signals our body is giving us to slow down. So, the body simply stops us in our tracks, puts us flat on our back, and provides us with no alternative but to slow down.

The body gives wise counsel. Pay close attention to its signals. Work with them as we have worked with feelings by slowing down, focusing your attention on the discomfort, and allowing inner guidance to arise.

EXERCISE

Signs, Symbols, and Pains

- Sit down comfortably and relax.
- Put your attention on your breath. Watch its natural rhythm — in and out, in and out.
- As your mind becomes totally relaxed and empty, scan the past few days and remember the last time you experienced a pain in your body while at work. Perhaps it was a neck pain, a backache, a pain in the arm, etc.
- Staying in that relaxed state, bring the pain back into the present, just for a short time, the duration of this exercise, and recreate that discomfort.
- With your mind at rest and your censoring mechanisms turned off, stay with the pain until an image, a word, or a phrase comes forth. Don't press for information, let it arise, or not arise, easily.
- If an image arises, carry on an inner dialogue with it to gain more information. If a word or phrase arises, ask the place in the body where the pain resides, "Tell me more," until no more information is forthcoming.
- In future, when you experience pain in your body at work stop as soon as possible, and begin the process described above.

Symbolism and the "Accidents" of Daily Life

Like the signals from our body, the accidents in our daily lives can be understood on the symbolic level. Though accidents, by definition, are not consciously intended, they can be seen as the result of unconscious intention. We can view accidents as another avenue over which the unconscious slips past the censor to deliver a symbolic message to the conscious mind.

Freud was very interested in the meaningfulness of what we call accidents. For him there were no accidents. If an outcome was not the result of conscious intention, then it was the outcome of unconscious intention. We now call this phenomena, the "Freudian slip," a misspoken word, which upon inspection can be understood as meaningful. For instance, I may intend to say to a student, "I'll have all these papers read by next week," but what actually I actually say is, "I'll have all these papers read by next month." At first, it appears I made a mistake, I misspoke. But upon further inspection it is clear that because I am so busy, I really don't want to read the papers until next month. Through the mistake, the hidden desire got through.

It is important to understand this phenomenon not as an "either or" choice. That it must either be a mistake, or it is symbolically true. It is both. The dichotomy is not necessary. It is a mistake at one level and true at another. It is more useful to look at the accident of speech, or any other kind of unintended event from both levels, the literal and the symbolic. In this way, we add to our knowledge of ourselves rather than limit it.

I was having a glass of wine and talking with a friend about a mutual friend who is going through a difficult period. She said, "Maybe I should offer Jack a session and help him work this stuff out." At that moment she reached for her glass, but knocked it over. The glass broke, and the wine spilled out. As we have similar perspectives on the symbolism of accidents, we looked at each other and laughed. We both felt the message was obvious. It brought forward what she knew very well but was suppressing for the moment in her desire to help her friend. It is not useful to offer people counseling. It needs to be requested to be truly helpful. To offer it is a waste, like spilling a fine wine.

Recently, I lost my wallet and my money clip. Also, recently, I've been struggling with my ego in my work. It seems to be a never-ending process. The desire to "get ahead," be recognized and successful, from an ego-feeding point of view, has been coming up.

When I worked with the symbolism of losing my wallet and money, its meaning came clear. I don't need representations of myself in the world to be satisfied and happy. The wallet was a symbol of my identity to others, and the money a symbol of material success. Losing them was a strong reminder that my journey is not about material success or recognition from others, it is about being and expressing Essence. It may include material success, and I welcome that, but ego is not at the center.

Evidently I didn't take the lesson in deeply enough, because I created yet another accident to reinforce this lesson. The next section of this book is on dreams. In it I discuss their symbolism and use as examples some recent dreams that had the same message for me as the accidental loss of my wallet and money. What happened was — believe it or not — I lost that whole section from my computer! I had to write it a second time. It made me frustrated and angry. But the truth is, it was not until that second writing that the message sunk in deeply enough, into my "guts," so that now it is a living truth in my life.

Try the following exercise and see if you can interpret the symbolic message of a minor accident in your work life.

EXERCISE

"Identifying the Meaning of an 'Accident' in Your Work Life"

- Sit down comfortably and relax.
- Put your attention on your breath. Watch its natural rhythm — in and out, in and out.
- As your mind becomes totally relaxed and empty, scan back on the past few days at work and remember something that happened that was unintended, a minor accident like losing a document or breaking something.
- Staying in that relaxed state, freely let associations come to you about what "meaning" there is in the accident.
- Keep allowing possibilities until one feels right. You will often experience yourself releasing a deep breath when the insight comes, or simply have an inner sense of knowing that the insight is "right on."
- If that confirmation of the deeper meaning does not come, that's fine. Do not push, rush, or press the process. Rushing and pressing activates the censoring aspect of the mind. Relaxing deactivates the censor.
- Let the question "perk" in your unconscious and go back to it occasionally during the day. Keep with it until the symbolic meaning comes to you.
- When "accidents" happen in future, stop and begin the above process in the moment.

Dreams

Since the beginning of time, dreams have been a rich source of symbolic information and guidance for humankind, all over the world. When we sleep, we have access to different levels of awareness than those available to us in the waking state. The censor is at rest, and all the sub-personalities and Essence have access to our consciousness. The distinction between the conscious and the unconscious fades.

In modern times, except for those doing dream work in psychotherapy, few of us are taking advantage of this wonderful source of information and guidance. To most, understanding our dreams seems a complicated, esoteric process that only an expert can manage.

Wrong. We can easily begin to mine the rich symbolism of our dreams to our benefit. Again, it is important to understand that there is no universal dictionary that we need to know which defines the meaning of dream symbols. The meanings of everyone's dream symbols vary. Yours are different than mine. You are the expert on the symbolism of your own dreams.

To tap the information your dreams hold for you, the first necessary step is to remember them. This is a major stumbling block for many people. Actually, remembering dreams is not as difficult as you may believe. It is similar to becoming physically fit. When we begin, we need to start gradually and slowly. If we continue, it soon becomes second nature.

If you do not remember your dreams, or if you think you don't dream, which is unlikely, begin by making a commitment to remembering them. Place a notebook or tape recorder by your bedside, and before you go to sleep, set an intention to wake up after a dream and write it down.

This is not easy, it breaks the comfort of continuous sleep and takes effort. But, like the early stages of a fitness program, the beginning is the most difficult period, requiring the most sacrifice and commitment. As the process becomes easier, your memory for dreams will improve, and you will not have to wake in the night to remember them.

Soon, you can write your dreams in the morning. After that, you won't need to write them at all, unless you wish to keep a dream record to study their evolution.

The most straightforward approach to dream interpretation is taught by Gayle Delaney, a therapist and writer. She has developed a simple method for interpreting the symbolism of dreams. For every major person, place, or thing that appears in your dreams, ask yourself, "What does this represent to me?" Bypassing the thinking process, allow the meaning associated with the symbol to come forward. Free associate to arrive at *your* meaning for that symbol. So, if a car appears in your dream, ask yourself, "What does a car mean to me?" If a tree appears, or your brother, or the corner grocery from childhood, ask, "What does that represent to me?"

The other night I dreamt that I was walking with my three brothers and a group of three attractive women appeared in front of us. I left my brothers, went to them, and began flirting. Then I was with one of the women, sitting across the table from her in a restaurant. I leaned over and kissed her. It felt very sexy and stimulating, and, at the same time, it felt empty and insubstantial, like being in lukewarm salt water.

As I worked with this dream, I saw that the major symbolic elements are my brothers, the group of women, the one woman, the table, the kiss, and how it felt. As I freely associated meaning for each, the symbolism was as follows:

My brothers represented for me, being "home," residing in Essence.

The women represented, for me, the seductive attraction of the sexual pleasure.

The individual woman in the restaurant represented the possibility of fulfilling that desire.

The table represented the barrier of social taboos.

The kiss represented overcoming the barriers and achieving sex for the pure pleasure of it.

The feeling from the kiss was the feeling of pleasure along with the feeling of emptiness. It represented to me the insubstantial and fleeting nature of ego pleasure.

The elements of the dream, taken together, brought me a powerful message. It reminded me that my real "home," the place of solid, enduring satisfaction, is in identification with Essence. The attractions and pleasures of the body and the ego feel good, but ultimately they don't satisfy me. What the dream teaches me about work is that for me to be really satisfied, I need to remember that the seduction of pleasures is nothing compared to expressing my Essence.

This dream, occurring at about the same time as the "accidental" loss of my wallet, reaffirms, with different symbols, through a different medium, the same message. My inner knowing has been very active, in both my sleeping and waking life, to communicate this important information.

There are other ways to work with dreams that you may find helpful. Fritz Perls, the founder of Gestalt psychology, used an effective approach to understanding the personal symbolic content of dreams, based on the dialogue method.

Using the Gestalt method, we enact the role of each of the major elements in the dream and have a conversation with it. For instance, for the dream I just presented, I engage in a dialogue with the woman sitting across from me in the restaurant. I ask, "What do you represent to me?," and she replies, "I represent the joy and pleasure of pure sexuality." I continue the dialogue and ask, "What is it that you can teach me?" She replies, "I can teach you that you love this joy and pleasure, and that it's not enough. In fact, it can get in the way of remembering who you are. That is what you truly love."

Another way to understand dreams is offered by Eugene Gendelin, the founder of Focusing, the approach to understanding our feelings in which we place our attention on the felt sense in the body, and let it speak to us. Transposing this method to dream work, we drop into the feeling tone of a dream, notice where the feeling resides in the body, and allow the body to interpret the symbolism.

Using this approach, I become the woman in my dream. I drop into what that feels like. At first, it is a generalized hot tingling sensation all over my body. Then, with close attention, I notice it to be strongest in the roof of my mouth. I focus my attention there, and it says to me, "I am the fire of pleasure. I can burn right through your mouth and into your brain. I can sear you. Be careful."

All methods of dream work bring us the same gift: increased self understanding and guidance.

EXERCISE

Dream Guidance

- Tonight place a notebook or tape recorder by your bed. Before you go to sleep, set an intention to awaken after a dream. When you realize you have been dreaming, wake up and record it.
- If it doesn't happen tonight, do it again tomorrow, continue until you are successful.
- In the morning, take out a piece of paper and fold it in half. Extract the major elements in your dream, and record them on the left side of the paper.
- If possible, have a helper ask you, "What does this represent to you?" for each entry. Respond freely, without thought or censorship, and have your helper write your response down next to each dream element, in the right hand column.
- If it is not possible to have a helper, simply do the process yourself.
- Look at the associations you have written on the right hand side of the paper. These are the meanings of your dream symbols.
- Link together these symbolic meanings in a natural way that produces a story or message for you.
- Ask yourself, "What guidance is in this for me? What guidance does it contain, if any, about my work?
- Now, using the Gestalt method, choose one of the elements in your dream, recorded on the left side of the paper, and have a dialogue with it. Ask it "What do you represent to me?" and continue with whatever other questions you may wish to ask.
- Enter into a dialogue with that element until you are satisfied that you have learned all you can learn from it for now.
- Finally, using the Focusing method, become one of the elements. Feel the body sense you have when you become that element.
- After a short while, notice if there is a specific place in your body where the felt sense is strongest. Put all of your attention there. Feel it deeply. Allow a word or phrase to emerge from that place that tells you more about the feeling.
- Ask that place in your body any questions you wish to ask it. Continue until you are satisfied that you have learned all you can for now.

- Put all these different sources of information together and notice the richness, understanding, and guidance that comes through one dream.

Intentional Symbol Systems

So far, we have spoken about symbols that come to us as unsolicited gifts; a message from our body, an accident, or a dream. We can, however, intentionally invite symbols into our lives to serve as a screen upon which to project our unconscious material and turn it into gold.

The best way to do this is through the use of an oracle, symbol systems that have been used for centuries to help people gain insight and clarity about themselves. The *Chinese Book of Changes*, the *I Ching,* is such an oracle. In it are 64 hexagrams or short chapters, each presented in symbolic language and made up of numerous references to natural phenomena such as lakes, mountains, the earth, fire, etc.

To use the *I Ching,* we randomly select a hexagram and look into it for guidance. The symbolic language of the oracle allows us to project our personal associations onto it and calls forth the inner knowing lying just below the surface of our awareness.

The Tarot also provides an excellent opportunity to work intentionally with symbols. As we discussed earlier, the Tarot is a set of 78 cards with visual symbols and descriptive words. We pick one randomly and look into it for guidance.

I use the cards often to help me in my work. Recently, I was having difficulty writing. I began to think, "I'll finish this chapter and take off a few weeks to rest." But I wasn't really clear. I consulted the Tarot with the intention of allowing it to help me better understand what I wanted to do.

The first card I drew had "Time and Space" written at the bottom, as well as images that I took to represent an understanding of time and space or wisdom. I interpreted the symbolism as an indication that the book is an authentic expression of my wisdom.

I then set the intention to get guidance regarding my wanting to take a long break after this chapter. I drew a card. On it I saw a bunch of jumbled objects and the word "Negativity." I understood this to mean that I wasn't stopping from a real need to rest, but out of some kind of negativity.

With some introspection, I could see that the interpretation this card brought forth from me was true. I was making the writing hard. Instead of focusing on the satisfaction and joy that writing brings me, I was focusing almost entirely on the difficulty.

Then I consulted the cards for guidance as to how I could shift my mental framework and continue writing. I drew a card that had a clown face on it and that said "Fool Child." I took this to mean that I need to hold the work more lightly and more playfully, rather than treat it as a chore to be finished.

Immediately, I felt released from the heaviness and no longer had the need to stop. The cards had been a way to draw on my inner wisdom and guide me forward in my work.

This same process of consulting the cards can be used between people and in groups. I have repeatedly seen people gain deep insight into their work through using the Tarot. I sometimes ask my clients to draw a card from the Tarot deck for guidance about a question that concerns them.

Not long ago I was working with a small professional business in this way. I asked each member of the five person staff to randomly select a card with the intention of getting information about what was going on for them in this group.

The first woman, a very upbeat and kind person, got the card "Anger." At first she said she didn't understand why she would draw such a card, it didn't fit her. Then she sat quietly and tears began to fall from her eyes. She spoke with great emotion about how she felt extremely overworked, and that she is both sad and angry about it. She had not been able to say this before or even allow herself to fully recognize it. It wasn't "nice," and she wanted her colleagues to "like her."

Rather than not liking her, the others were grateful. They thanked her for her words, saying they didn't know the depth of her feeling and were eager to help out and relieve some of the burden.

The next person to choose a card drew another difficult symbol, "Oppression." Her first reaction was similar to her colleague, "This doesn't apply to me." Then, as she began to explore the meaning more deeply, she said "Yeah, the truth is, I am feeling oppressed." She had come from living a free and easy life in a rural setting and was now in an urban office with schedules and pressures she didn't like.

Finally, the boss said, "You know, I feel opprressed, too. The pace around here is killing me. We need to slow down." The Tarot had loosened the stranglehold of the office culture and allowed them to truly recognize their feelings and share them.

Barbara Lee, my partner in the seminar business, an artist, and symbolist, has recently developed a set of cards for use as projective devices, specifically designed to gain information about work. It is called the *Rekindling the Spirit in Work Deck*. We have begun to use the cards in our seminars with great success. The cards contain collaged images and phrases. They bring forward our unconscious feelings and insights about work.

A gifted bodyworker, who has recently moved to Hawaii, was using the *Rekindling the Spirit in Work Deck*. He told us that since he has moved, he has had a hard time making a living. One of the cards he drew contained the phrase "Let yourself be influential." Sam read it as, "Let yourself be influenced." When he saw the difference between what he read, and what it actually said, Sam realized consciously how out of control and helpless he actually felt. He also realized that he wasn't helpless and that if he were patient and allowed his work to grow at a natural and healthy pace, he was fully capable of prospering.

Whether we go to signs and symbols intentionally, or just watch them unfold naturally in our daily lives, they are full of valuable information. They can be a source of profound help and guidance in maintaining the dynamic balance to express our spirit in work.

8 DAILY LIFE
STAYING TUNED & BALANCED

The Self that dwells in everyone should be worshiped constantly.
Until there is worship of the Self
no matter how many churches we visit,
no matter how many temples we visit,
no matter how many mosques we visit,
there is no real peace.
When we worship the Self,
that is when we attain happiness, true contentment.

GURUMAYI

Daily practice is consistent attention to the positive development of each element of our being. Using the integral model, this includes the mind, body, emotions, and spirit.

Daily practice is exercise. Most of us are familiar with exercise at the body level: walking, swimming, hiking, push-ups, sit-ups, and so on. An integrated program of daily practice also includes exercise for the mind, emotions, and spirit.

The purpose of daily practice is to gain strength, flexibility, and balance. In the face of the pace and stress of our lives, identifying with Essence is very challenging. It takes the qualities developed through daily practice to remember who we are and express it in our work.

Without an integrated program of exercise/practice at all levels, we forget that our true nature is Essence and, under pressure, become identified with one or another of our sub-personalities. We get anxious and retreat into old patterns. We further identify with other fearful sub-personalities and fall into a downward spiral.

The sub-personalities are not big enough, or strong enough, to integrate all of who we are, as well as cope with the demands of our work. As a result, we are often in conflict with ourselves and others. The outcome is we are less effective in our work, and far less satisfied.

Good intentions are not enough. Just as the desire to be physically fit without the physical workout will not produce fitness; wanting to identify with Essence without consistent daily practice will not produce that identification.

Similarly, wanting work to be an expression of Essence is not sufficient. Inevitably, we will be thrown off balance and into identification with smaller parts of ourselves unless we have built strength and balance through an integrated program of daily practice.

To discuss daily practice in greater depth, we will use the integral model as our guide. We will consider the types of practices that develop each aspect. It should be remembered, however, that any division of ourselves is somewhat artificial. We cannot be divided neatly into parts. All aspects of ourselves are interelated and, in a sense, mingle with each other. They cannot be entirely separated.

For example, exercising the body, also develops the mind, the emotions, the spirit. This is true for all levels, practice in one will strengthen the others. To be fully developed, however, to have the flexibility and balance to be Essence in our work, we must develop all levels of our being.

The Body

The element of an integrated daily practice with which we are most familiar is physical exercise; walking, running, swimming, bicycling, aerobics, weight training, and so on. These activities activate the body into vigorous movement, developing muscle tone, stimulating the internal organ systems, and cleansing the body of toxins.

There are many forms of physical exercise. It is a simple matter of choosing the one you like, one which suits your life style, and doing it. There are numerous books, classes, and teachers to support this effort.

It is important to select a physical exercise you enjoy, one which you find pleasurable and rewarding. If it feels good, you are likely to continue exercising. If it doesn't, you are likely to quit.

The "No pain, no gain" school of exercise has done a disservice. People who believe this maxim expect that they are not supposed to enjoy their practice. Eventually, most of these people quit. Few of us will choose to regularly make our life more painful than it already is.

It's far more valuable to exercise at a level of effort that is comfortable and do it on a steady basis. It is helpful to remember our purpose. We are not trying to qualify for the Olympics, we are tuning, balancing, and strengthening ourselves to live a more satisfying life.

Diet is also an important component of daily practice. Diet is, of course, directly related to health and well being. It is central to maintain the body in a state that keeps us physically, mentally, and emotionally clear.

We do not have to be expert nutritionists to know how to eat well for health. All we need do is bring awareness to the process. Since pleasure is so central to eating, and since eating is so deeply enmeshed in habit, bringing awareness to the process is not easy.

The key is developing an awareness of the effect of each food on us after we eat it. Our awareness regarding eating is generally undeveloped. We usually limit ourselves to a narrow range of discrimination; do we "like it" or not, does it "taste good" or not, is it "easy to prepare" or not, do "they say" it's healthy or not. How a food actually effects our overall state of being is seldom the concern.

The effect food has on us is the central question in a healthful diet. The most important skill in creating a healthful personal diet is observation.

This is the way ancient peoples tested their environment for safe foods. They used an experimental model. Someone ate a small amount of a naturally growing substance and waited. If they felt good later, the food was considered healthy. If they felt bad, it was unhealthy.

All we need do to bring a healthful diet into our lives is apply this experimental process to our normal eating behavior. We eat our food and notice how does it feel afterwards. Immediately afterwards, one half hour later, two hours later, the next day.

If we watch closely and refine our attention, we can design our own perfect diet by eating those foods that feel good. Foods that cause a lot of strain put us off balance and in a reactive mode. They do not support the inner state necessary for maintaining an identification with Essence.

In general, "light" food supports us in maintaining a balanced inner state, i.e., fresh fruit, vegetables, and grains, as well as a low intake of meat, fat, sugar, and milk products. It is important to understand that this is not a moral issue, religious issue, or a matter of doing what someone else believes is correct. Check it out for yourself. Eat a steak and notice how you feel afterwards, the next few hours, and the next day. If you feel heavy and sluggish, its not supporting you. Eat rice with vegetables, and notice how you feel later. If you feel light and comfortable, it is supporting you. You are in charge, you make the decisions based on your understanding of your own body.

Besides what we eat, the amount and way we eat is also important. I have noticed that if I eat until I am "full," then later I feel over stuffed. I'm uncomfortable, sluggish, and irritable.

There is a lag time between the sensation of fullness and the actual time at which we have had a sufficient amount of food. So, for my well being, I have learned to stop eating before I am "full," knowing that the sensation of satisfaction will come later, in about twenty minutes or less.

Eating slowly and chewing thoroughly is helpful for the digestive process and also cuts down on the lag time between when one stops eating and when one feels satisfied. If we eat slowly enough, the lag is eliminated, and we feel in the moment when we have actually had enough.

The way we breathe and the quality of the air we breath are important factors in our health. Breath is perhaps our most primary connection to the life force. For a millennium, in the East, yogis have put breath work at the center of their daily practice. In Sanskrit this is called *pranayana*.

We need not be yogis or experts to use the natural breathing process to support us in staying identified with Essence. There are simple things we can do to improve the way we take in the breath of life. By far the most important element is awareness of the process.

Because breathing is natural and automatic, we seldom honor the process. Yet because it is so critical to our well being, it deserves care and attention.

Healthy breathing, in general, is steady and deep. Shallow or constricted breathing will negatively effect your health and inner state. It will tend to move you toward a reactive mode rather than into balanced wholeness.

From time to time, put your attention on your breathing. Notice if there is constriction, notice if the breath is shallow. If you see that you are holding your breath, or that it is shallow, the act of directing your attention to the breath alone will begin to transform it into a healthier pattern. Healthful breathing is not so much a matter of effort, as it is intention.

Set an intention to breath deeply and easily. Every time you notice constriction, simply reaffirm your intention. Allow deep relaxing breaths to come freely.

There is a cultural norm against allowing deep releasing breaths to occur spontaneously. It is viewed as something like belching in public. The taboo has carried over into our private lives, so that we have conditioned ourselves against allowing deep releasing breaths to come in their natural course. Releasing breaths are very healthful and contribute to our overall state of balance. They act as a release valve for tension and anxiety. Do not buy into this counterproductive etiquette. When a releasing breath comes, allow it.

The most healthful breathing is in and out through the nose. It is the natural way to breathe — the way babies and animals do. Those who have studied the breathing process for thousands of years, the yogis of India, have determined that the warming and cleansing effect of bringing the air in through the nose is most healthful. Also, after one begins to breath this way, it becomes obvious that it is more relaxing and free, allowing consistently deeper, fuller, more satisfying breathing. Experiment and see what works for you.

Mind

The most potent practice for developing strength, flexibility, and balance in the mind is meditation. There are many forms of meditation and each has a different purpose and method. The form of meditation that is most relevant and helpful to us is Mindfulness Meditation.

The technique is simple. Awareness is focused on the breath, watching the breath as it goes in and comes out. When we are aware that the attention has wandered from the breath, we notice where it has wandered and bring the attention back to the breath.

This straightforward technique is extremely powerful for observing and beginning to understand more precisely how the mind works. Usually, it becomes obvious that the mind runs here, there, and everywhere, like a playful monkey. It plans, and worries, and plays, and regrets, skipping from one place to the next, with lightning speed, all day long.

One moment we are focused on our work, the next we are worrying about money. Just as quickly we are thinking about dinner, and then the kids.

While this is happening, we are seldom clearly aware of it. Rather, it is happening to us. Mostly the mind jumps from thought to thought, while we do not consciously, with awareness, choose to make the jumps. It is as if we are on a roller coaster, and the curves and drops just keep coming. Often, it appears that we are the victims not the masters of the mind.

For example, Ralph is working on a report at the office. He remembers he has to take the car in at 5:00 P.M. for a brake job. Then his mind skips to the last time he repaired the car and how expensive it was. He begins to worry about not having enough money. "How are we going to pay for Janie's first year of college, plus all our normal expenses?" Then he starts questioning if he really is paid well enough for all the hard work he does. He wonders if Frank, his co-worker is overpaid. "Frank doesn't do half of what I do, and he makes more than me." Then he becomes angry and resentful about the low pay for long hours. Ralph ends up furious at his boss and his company. The whole process occurred in the mind, with no change in the outside environment, and took less than one minute.

Sound familiar? It happens to us all the time. Our mind skips from one subject to the next, brings forth the accompanying emotions, and the rest of us goes along for the ride. We are not in control of that movement. This the nature of the unexamined mind. From this place, identification with Essence cannot last.

Mindfulness meditation, as a daily practice, can change this. We can shift from servants of the mind, to its master. We watch the breath and notice where the mind moves. As we continue the practice, we begin to see the patterns of the mind and understand them. The awareness itself shifts the patterns from uncontrolled leaps to slower movements, in which we participate more fully in choosing the direction and location of the movement.

The meditation is a microcosm of our nonmeditative, normal waking state. We are doing something, or thinking about something, and the mind wanders. Usually we are not aware of it. But, with time and mindfulness practice, we become aware of the wandering mind and learn to bring it back to the present.

Then, when we are writing the report at the office, and the mind wanders to the brake job, we know it. We are aware of that movement, not unconscious bystanders to it. We can choose to continue to move the attention in that direction, or we can bring it back to the report.

The following exercise includes step by step instructions for the practice of mindfulness meditation.

EXERCISE

"Mindfulness Meditation"

- Sit in a quiet place in a comfortable position and close your eyes.
- Focus your attention on your breath.
- Without changing the natural rhythm of your breath, put your attention on the movement of the breath as it goes in and out, in and out.
- When you notice that your mind has wandered from the breath, notice where it has moved to, and bring it gently back to the breath. Continue to focus on the breath as it comes in and goes out.
- Again, when you notice your attention has wandered from the breath, notice where it has wandered, and bring it gently back to the breath.
- Do this five minutes to an hour at a time, as often as you like, at least once or twice a day.

Emotions

There are two ways to work with emotions as a daily practice. The first is an extension of mindfulness meditation. It involves noticing not only where the mind wanders, but also the emotional states associated with the wandering mind.

In general, emotions accompany thought. When you think about your wife, you may become glad, you may become sad. When you think of your job, you may become elated, you may become angry. The mindfulness meditation can be extended to include noticing the emotional state that accompanies thought.

Through noticing these patterns and understanding their movement, we gain freedom and balance. We achieve at least partial control over the effects of our emotional states.

Another form of daily practice, focused on the emotional level, is the feeling work we have discussed throughout the book and explained in depth in Chapter Four. This takes the mindfulness approach to emotions even farther into discovering the source of the emotional reaction and releasing it.

The following exercise reiterates a process presented in Chapter Four. It is a method for releasing ourselves from the discomfort of a constricting emotional state, as well as letting go of identifications at the sub-personality level.

EXERCISE

Emotional Release

- Notice when an emotional state is manifesting as a strong feeling.
- Allow the feelings to be there without denying, pushing them away or avoiding them.
- Progressively, open more fully to the feeling. Notice the place in your body where the physical sensation is most prominent.
- Letting go of the focus on the emotions themselves, focus all your attention on the physical sensation.
- Amplify the feeling tone. Let it get bigger.
- Step in and "become the feeling."
- With your mind and thoughts "on holiday," allow a word or image to "bubble up" to you, directly from that place in your body.

- If you get an image, consider that the image is a symbol of a sub-personality that is creating this feeling and:

  a. Internally, ask the symbol what it wants. Let the symbol, not your mind, reply.

  b. Now ask it what it really, really needs, and let the symbol reply.

- If a symbol doesn't come to you, treat the physical place in your body where the felt sense resides as the spokesperson for the sub-personality, and ask that place what it wants. Then ask it what it really needs.

- Do this all very slowly.

- When you receive the information from the symbol, or from your body, really allow your whole self to soak it in. Go slowly and relax. Allow spontaneous deep breathing to occur. This is a sign that it has reached the body level of understanding.

- Allow the image or body part that is representative of a sub-personality to speak to the bigger part of you, your Essence, and ask it to see this smaller part's need for what has been identified above.

- Then, gracefully shift into an identification with Essence by using your affirmation. From an identification with Essence, acknowledge that the need of the sub-personlaity is seen and understood.

- Allow a dialogue to develop between the sub-personality that has the need, and Essence, that sees and understands it.

- This exercise can be done, as part of your daily practice, as often as you feel it useful, whenever a strong emotional state comes up.

Spirit

Spiritual practice is any exercise that acknowledges, connects, and identifies us with the Divine. We have already learned one of the most powerful spiritual practices there is, the affirmation of Essence.

By repeating the affirmation, "I am_____, (filling in the blank with the Essence quality you discovered in yourself in Chapter One), you are affirming your identity with the Divine. There is no daily practice more effective in developing your spiritual self than identifying with the part of you that is a reflection the Great Mystery.

Also, any form of devotion is spiritual practice. Prayer, acknowledging our gratitude to the Creator for all our gifts and blessings as well as asking for direction and guidance, is a powerful form of spiritual practice. All prayer connects us with spirit, builds strength, and keeps spirit in the center of our lives.

Many types of meditation are spiritual practice. Repeating the name of God, or aspects of the Divine, in any language, is the spiritual practice called mantra meditation. This method, popularized in the West by the well known Indian teacher Maharishi Mahesh Yogi through Transcendental Meditation or TM, is mantra meditation.

Also, any form of meditation that releases the practioner from the grip of the rational mind and opens one into the experience of the formless is spiritual practice. This is done through deep self-relaxing into a trance-like state and remaining in that state for the duration of the meditation. Achieving and abiding in the formless is a way of connecting and identifying with the Divine.

EXERCISE

Mantra Meditation

- Sit in a quiet place, in a comfortable position, and close your eyes.
- Repeat to yourself the word One (an aspect of the Divine).
- Continue to repeat the word One, at your own pace. It is best to proceed slowly and easily, maintaining your attention on the internal sound of the word.
- When you notice that your mind has wandered from the sound, without judgement or blame, bring yourself back to repeating the word One.
- Continue to focus on the sound of One repeating it silently to yourself.
- Again, when you notice your attention has wandered from the sound One, without judgement or blame, bring yourself back to repeating the word.
- Do this five minutes to an hour at a time, as often as you like, at least once or twice a day.

Conclusion and Sample Practice

It may appear a bit overwhelming at first to include in your daily practice exercises at all four levels of our being. With time, however, you will notice it is very comfortable and manageable. You will come to enjoy your daily practice for the peace, balance, and harmony it brings into your life, as well as the increased level of satisfaction into your work.

A sample program of an integrated daily practice is as follows:

◆ Physical exercise, twenty minutes to one hour a day, three to five times per week. Light, healthful diet, and attention to the breath throughout the day.

◆ Emotional release work throughout the day, whenever strong feelings arise.

◆ Meditation, twice a day, once in morning once in evening, before meals, fifteen to thirty minutes each. Including:

- *First five to ten minutes, any emotional release work that hasn't already been done.*
- *Five to ten minutes, repetition of your affirmation, I Am (Essence Quality).*
- *Final five to ten minutes, Mindfulness Meditation.*

III
THE WORKPLACE

9 ❧ FROM FAMIILY TO WORKPLACE HEALING OURSELVES AT WORK

If you cannot get rid of the family skeleton,
you may as well make it dance.

GEORGE BERNARD SHAW

The workplace, especially the work group, provides us with the opportunity to heal our childhood wounds. The work group replicates, in many ways, our family-of-origin. At work, as in our first family, we are in close proximity to others, share ideas, attitudes, beliefs, and it is a place where we have strong emotional bonds. Perhaps most importantly, work, like our first families, is the source of our sustenance and survival. Feelings that come up in the workplace often duplicate the ones we first felt in our family-of-origin.

The intensity of emotional relationships with others in the workplace, both loves and hates, is matched only by the emotional intensity of our childhood reactions in the family. The similarity between the family-of-origin and the work group is central to understanding our feelings about work, and transforming our blocks into aids for growth.

Though it has become appallingly clear that there is widespread physical abuse of children in our society, still, most childhood wounding is at the emotional level. Because the work group replicates the depth of emotions we had in our original family, it is in the workplace that it is possible to reexperience the pain of our original wounding and release it.

As long as the wounding remains below the surface, constrictions in the feelings, and the behavior it causes, inhibit our ability to be who we truly are. Each time we release a constricting pattern, we are more free and able to identify with Essence.

The main reason the workplace is problematic is not our

FROM FAMILY TO WORKPLACE   115

lack of technical competency, but the emotional entanglements in which we find ourselves trapped. The theme of this chapter is that this discomfort is also an opportunity. Like the Chinese pictogram, danger and opportunity are represented in the same character.

The emotional turmoil we experience at work is painful. Often what is happening is that feelings surrounding old wounds are being pushed into our consciousness by the present situation to be reexperienced so that they can be healed. Feelings come to the surface to be healed.

Sometimes when I am working with an organization, we get "stuck." It feels like wading through emotional cobwebs. No one knows where to turn without getting further enmeshed. In those moments I have said, "This is hard, and it seems like an uncomfortable problem at this moment, on this particular day. But, when you look at it more closely, does it feel familiar? Is the feeling tone in your body something you have experienced before? Has each of us felt this feeling in other groups at other times? Does it go all the way back to your childhood?"

Invariably it does. If people are willing to open to the sensations within them, they see the replication of a pattern that began in their family-of-origin and has continued throughout their lives. They experience the same core set of difficult feelings, while the actual external problems and the people involved change in the various work groups they have participated in. The magic is, the exact right people come together and create the situation of reproducing the dynamics of each of their personal histories, for each other, so they can be reexperienced and released.

If we do not release the pain of childhood wounding, it remains beneath the surface, like a bed of nails below the mattress. We may get used to it, but it's not fun. If we really allow ourselves to feel the emotional discomforts at work, all the way to the body level, we can then reconnect with the original events that caused our wounding. Most often this will have first occurred in the family setting. Through developing awareness, and the willingness to feel it, we will naturally release without effort or strain our blocks to rewarding work.

The typical response to interpersonal discomfort at work is to deny that there is a problem or "solve it" at the external level. This is why the pain of childhood wounding is still alive in us. We deny the truth of our feelings because it is too uncomfortable; we "stuff it" below the surface of our consciousness; or, we intellectually "figure out" a way to "solve the problem" in the world. That is, we manipulate the environment for the purpose of eradicating the visible source of our discomfort.

Unfortunately, denying a problem or solving it on the external level when its origin is internal does not work. It may "fix" things for awhile, but inevitably, when a similar situation arises, the wounded button will be pressed again. The painful feeling will re-emerge, offering us yet another opportunity to practice the three Rs.

> *Recognize it,*
> *Reexperience it,*
> *and Release it.*

Over the past few years a friend of mine, Art, has told me the story of his chronic dissatisfaction with one of his business partners, who is also a childhood friend. He both loves and hates Peter. The relationship has so deteriorated they are dissolving the partnership.

There are many specific issues they disagree about, but Art says, "The bottom line is I feel like he is taking advantage of me. He's not doing his share, he's not paying the bills on time, and it pisses me off. Why should I have to carry him?"

Just the other day we were together and Art was commiserating with me about all this. Because I knew him as a kid, knew his family, I had an insight. I said, "Does this whole thing feel familiar? Does Peter remind you of your little brother, whom you felt took advantage of you, and whom you felt you carried throughout your childhood?"

He went silent in apparent recognition and understanding. Art was reexperiencing at work, over and over again, the pain he had with his little brother at home. It kept coming to the surface to be healed.

EXERCISE

Tracing Interpersonal Problems at Work to Childhood Wounding

- Be seated in a comfortable position. Allow yourself to relax. Bring your attention to the breath. Without any attempt to change it, simply focus on the breath, watching the natural rhythm of its in and out flow. Exhale any tension with the exhaling breath. Relax your whole body, section by section, from the feet to the head.
- Bring into your consciousness the interpersonal discomfort you are experiencing at work.
- Focus your attention on that feeling. Allow the feeling fully in.
- Notice where in your body you feel it most. Put all your attention on that spot. Let it become all of who you are.
- Now, detaching your mind, as if it were on vacation, let the body itself speak to you. Or let an image emerge that represents that feeling. Let the body or the image bubble up words to your consciousness describing the essential feeling you are experiencing.
- Ask that part in your body or the image, "Where do you come from?" Wait patiently for a response.
- Now ask, "What in my childhood are you connected to?" Wait for an answer.
- Sit quietly with this information, asking any other questions you wish, but, most importantly, allow in the knowing that these insights carry.

Reexperiencing the Pain

The thesis of this book is that if we understand and identify with who we are, then what we do as our work will flow out naturally. To identify with Essence, we have to be in a continual process of clearing away barriers to that identification. The blocks to our knowing ourselves as Essence stem from the wounding we have received in our lives, and the defenses we developed to protect ourselves. These defense mechanisms are useful. But, when they continue to live on beyond the time they are functional, they are a hindrance.

Continually engaging in a process of clearing away the barriers is essential. This "clear space" is the ground from which we can truly experience ourselves as Essence and our work as its expression. The opportunities to do this clearing come up in numerous ways every day at work.

When we feel uncomfortable at work, we need to dive directly into it and feel the feelings. It is the time to recognize that we have the opportunity to reexperience the original pain and release it. This process frees us from the unconscious blocks that keep us enslaved in unrewarding patterns and continually reexperiencing the same emotional dissatisfaction at work.

I was reading a novel the other day. The sage advice to the hero from his grandfather was, "When you got a problem my boy, or when somethin' feels bad, face it right away. Don't avoid it, or it'll come back to haunt you." This is precisely the case with clearing emotional blocks in the workplace. Each time one comes up "face it right away." Don't avoid it, or like the South, it will rise again. This is one of the most important daily practices we can do to make work a more rewarding experience.

Last year, when I was still a university chairperson, we had a meeting of our department to "vision and plan our future." It was a wonderful meeting, uplifting in many ways. We shared our dreams for our group and began the nuts and bolts planning to make them real. Near the end, one faculty member expressed his dissatisfaction. "I'm tired of this planning to plan." He said, "When are we going to really get something done?"

Surprisingly, I blew my stack. I said to him, "What do you mean, 'when are we going to get something done?' What do you think we've been doing for the past eight hours. What do you think we've been doing for the past eight years?"

As the chairperson of the department, I was defensive and felt personally attacked. I knew I was overreacting but in the moment I had no insight into what was really going on inside.

With more time, and the imperative to take my own counsel, I opened to my feelings. I stopped projecting my discomfort onto my colleagues. "What unhealed wound inside is being activated by this interaction," I asked myself?

As is often the case, it was not difficult to understand once I was willing to feel. The part of me that has wanted to satisfy others had been touched and hurt. The "pleaser" sub-personality was still alive, though it had long since outlived its usefulness.

I later apologized to the individual involved and the department suffered no visible negative consequences from the incident. But it was a wonderful learning for me that with only a minimum of pressure from my fellow faculty's comments, the wound screamed out.

In all probability I will experience this pain again. From time to time the discomfort arising from this inner sense that I am not enough will return, until I feel it deeply enough and finally let it go.

We have all experienced not only our own overreactions, but the overreactions of others at work. We make a comment, and someone "blows up." Their energy is out of proportion with the original comment. It comes from a place within the respondent that is hurt and festering. If we remember that others are often reacting from their wounds, and not take their response as personal to us, it makes others' reactions in the work group more understandable and work a more pleasant experience.

Because my sore spot was touched at that meeting, and I was eventually willing to feel it, I was able to identify its source in a way I never had before. It is like someone touching your body and you discover a very painful spot that you weren't aware of until it was touched.

Workplace Issues & Family-of-Origin Dynamics

Many issues originating in family-of-origin dynamics surface in the workplace. Some of the strongest and most difficult to deal with are feelings around authority and the people in authority.

Most of us have unresolved feelings about authority. As children we are dependent upon adults for survival and love. The adults in our lives can use or abuse this responsibility. If the responsibility is abused, the child will suffer beyond the moment, into the future. One form of this is the construction of a subservient, rebellious, or negative attitude toward people in authority. Any significant adult in a childs' life, particularly parents, relatives, and teachers, can easily, even unintentionally, abuse their authority, and leave the child emotionally wounded.

In my experience with organizations, most of the problems in the workplace are fundamentally issues around authority. "Who is in charge, who is the boss," and most importantly "who tells who what to do." Feelings and strong reactions to our bosses, the major authority figures in our lives after parents and teachers, are recurrent. Feelings about our subordinates, those for whom we are the boss, also bring forth unresolved feelings around authority.

As boss, we are the parents and those we supervise are the children. If we do not consciously examine the process, we tend to direct with a style similar to our parents' leadership in the home. As subordinate, we tend to react to our bosses as we did to our parents when we were children. In either case, because of the parallel between the family-of-origin and the workplace, work brings up the feelings we had as children. If those feelings hurt in childhood, unless they have been healed since, they will still hurt today.

With peers and co-workers, authority issues also arise. In the case of peers, some are "more equal" than others. We often replicate our power struggles with brothers, sisters, and friends in the work group. Older brothers, stronger sisters, and just plain bullies have had their effect on us. The aspects of these relationships that were hurtful in childhood may be reexperienced through our relations with peers and co-workers.

Like most of us, I have had trouble in relationships with co-workers. Individually, my relations with co-workers have tended to be pleasant, but in a group they are sometimes uncomfortable. I have felt disempowered and vulnerable in group meetings.

When I examine this feeling more closely, from the inside out, the origin of the feelings is not difficult to find. The pattern, and the feeling tone associated with it, replicate my childhood family experience.

As the youngest son in a family of two parents and four brothers, my eldest brother being fifteen years older than I, and my closest brother in age eight years older, what I said in the family circle didn't count for much. Meetings with my co-workers and supervisors simulated the family dinner table of my childhood.

Going back, I reexperienced the sense of deep frustration I felt at not being able to influence the direction of important decisions in my life.

Since I had not reexperienced and released this feeling of powerlessness before, it reappears in the now until I understand and release it.

Transactional Analysis

Eric Berne developed a model that is helpful in understanding social behavior. It is called Transactional Analysis and has applications for healing family-of-origin wounding that arises at work. Berne simply and eloquently used the roles we have been talking about to look at the relationships between people; Parent, Adult, and Child. The Parent role emphasizes relations in which you exert power over another. The Child role emphasizes subservience to authority. The Adult role emphasizes equal and cooperative power relations with others.

If we have unfinished feelings about authority, we will generally play them out at work by adopting a Parent or Child role instead of an Adult role. Because we are, in fact, adults, these roles are incongruent with who we really are. We are not parents and children to each other, we are adults. The incongruence of being an adult and being in a Parent-Child relationship with another adult is out of balance and unhealthy.

Adult-to-Adult role relationships, in Berne's model, creates a context for satisfying work. If we feel ourselves a child or anothers' master, in the long run, it diminishes the pleasure and productivity of the relationship.

Our feeling about money is another important work-related issue with seeds in the past and difficulty in the present. Seldom are either the poor, the rich, or the in-between relaxed and easy about money.

The money issue reactivates childhood difficulties surrounding whether we felt there was enough money, or more importantly, whether there was "enough" to support our continued existence. To a child, this is a core survival issue that can be frightening. Feelings about money are very basic, strong, and deep.

After mother's breast, the family nest, and school, the workplace provides our direct link to survival. It is closely associated with our perceived ability to sustain ourselves, to simply stay alive. Money is the medium through which we think we survive.

We became sensitive to money issues in our family-of-origin. As our parents also had wounding around money and "enoughness," our first information on the subject was likely to have been tinged with fear and limitation. Our cares and fears about money in our work is imbedded in this unconscious web.

When we are uncomfortable about money, it is seldom for the reason we think. The surface problem is rooted to a deeper source. When we are worried that we are not paid enough, we think that in itself is the cause of our discomfort. The pay, and our concern about it, are not the source of our discomfort. The source lies in our fear that we will not survive. If we feel our feelings fully, we will sense the buried pain; a quiet strong fear that if we don't earn enough we will, at least symbolically, be obliterated.

The most powerful antidote to our worries about money is faith. If we are blessed with faith, there is little stress about money. Some people never worry over money, knowing they will have enough and always do. Others worry about money all their lives yet have never missed a meal, slept in the rain, or lacked for what they need. The Persian poet Rumi alluded to this when he wrote of cows who fattened every day in the field but every night became skinny over the worry of not seeing the grass.

I know that in my life, when I open to the faith that there will always be enough for me, the whole issue of money, work, the willingness to take risks and change becomes easier and lighter.

Deeply rooted in our family-of-origin dynamics is the unwillingness and fear to be who we truly are at work. Because, for most of us, being all of who we were as children was not acceptable to our parents, we are afraid to fully be ourselves at work. If we were criticized, punished, or not supported for living from Essence in childhood, we are unlikely to do so as adults in the workplace.

Another chronic discomfort many of us feel about work that originates in family-of-origin dynamics is the apparent contradiction between our desire for freedom and our need for security. Many of us dislike being a cog in a hierarchical organizational machine. In that setting, bosses have a good deal of real power over the quality of our workday. We long to be free and in control of our own lives.

On the other hand, we are afraid of independence because it appears to lack the security of a steady paycheck. Thus, the tension. We want freedom and we want security. We have learned they do not go together. It's one or the other.

In fact, security and freedom are not mutually exclusive. It is possible to have both. The way to have both is not to make these qualities incompatible in our minds but to allow them to live in harmony within us. If we believe we can have both, we can.

Continuing to work out of childhood programming and allowing that to determine what is possible, is very limiting. To the extent that we believe we are limited, we will be limited. To the extent we allow ourselves to feel the feeling tone of our limitations and see into their source, we can release them. We can integrate what we previously believed were incompatible qualities and be whole at work.

The following exercise is similar to *Holding Both*, presented in Chapter Two.

EXERCISE

Reconciling Apparent Contradictions

- Be seated in a comfortable position. Allow yourself to relax. Bring your attention to the breath. Without any attempt to change it, simply focus on the breath, watching the natural rhythm of its in and out flow. Exhale any tension with the exhaling breath. Relax your whole body, section by section, from the feet to the head.
- Allow yourself to let in a contradiction you are experiencing around work. Slowly, giving everything lots of time, identify the different

elements.

- Let yourself focus your attention first on the feeling tone of one element. Allow the feeling in fully.
- Now, focus your attention on the feeling tone of the second element. Allow the feeling in fully.
- Now, put one quality in each hand. Put your arms straight out in front of you and feel the qualities. Let your arms and hands move up and down, as if feeling the weight in each.
- Instead of choosing between the two, consider the possibility of holding both. Allow them to co-exist. Let both be there without having to do anything.
- How does that feel?
- Now, allow a symbol to arise for each.
- Let the two parts or their symbols talk to each other and listen to each others' needs.
- Go slowly and give this process plenty of time. Let your thinking be at rest and allow the symbols or elements in your hands to talk and make their own peace.
- When you are complete, return your attention to your breath.
- When you are ready, open your eyes.

Understanding Work Groups

"Watch what they do not what they say." If we observe the behavior of a work group, focusing on the patterns of interaction between people, rather than getting lost in their words, we can see the "story behind the story." Most often, the story behind the story is the repetition of family patterns in the workplace. In fact, if we develop an eye to see in this way, it becomes clear that most interactions between people at work are extensions of patterns developed long ago in the family setting repeated in the present. Family-of-origin dynamics are the basis of workplace dynamics.

As we have seen, in most work groups, someone takes the role of father, generally an older male who has formal authority, a boss. Also, someone takes the role of mother, usually a woman with seniority who has a nurturing character and tends to the emotional well-being of the group.

The role of the children is assumed by employees who have no

formal authority and accept their disempowered status as legiti-
mate. They consciously or unconsciously define themselves as dependent.

In the complex hierarchical structures of the corporate workplace,
identities are not static. Many people act out roles as both parents
and children. We are parents in the interpersonal dynamics of some
groups, and children in the dynamics of others. We may take the
role of sibling with our co-workers, parent to those we manage,
and child to those in authority.

Some years ago I was working with a small sales organization.
During a group meeting, the owner/boss became involved in a
conversation with his sales manager and bookkeeper. What I noticed, when I dropped below the content of the conversation, "behind the story," was that in this discussion about vacation periods,
all three were playing out their family dynamics. The situation was
actually a father and two daughters engaged in a power struggle.
The sisters, the sales manager and bookkeeper, were vying for dad's
approval. Each was trying to please and convince him, to win his
love and get her way.

Cappie and Laura each used a strategy with her boss that she
had learned with her father. Laura's pattern of response to the boss/
father followed the pattern, "No, I can't do it and I'll tell you why.
I'm already exhausted from sacrificing myself for you and the rest
of the family. You should love me and let me have my way, because
I do so much for you."

The other "sister," Cappie, repeated her own pattern with the
father/boss. Her story was different yet had the same intention.
"Yes, I can do it and I'll tell you why. It's because I'm so intelligent
I can always find a way to solve your problems. Because I'm so
smart and always help you, you should love me and let me have
my way."

The boss' pattern with his subordinates followed the patriachal
model he learned from his midwestern father. His chorus was, "I
want it done, I want it done right, and this is how I want you to do
it. If you do it my way, I will love you, and give you what you
want."

To an observer only following the surface story, the family dynamic was not apparent. It appeared to be a discussion of vacation time. But at the energetic level it was uncomfortable, stiff, convoluted, and old. The energy was out of proportion to the actual subject. When this happens, people are usually playing out roles and blocks that reach back into their personal histories.

There is a mysterious and magical phenomenon that unites us with the correct others, to play out our family-of-origin dynamics at work. In this case, the women had the opportunity to use the same strategies with their boss, to win his favor, as they did with their father. The boss' style was perfect for allowing the two women to play out their ingrained patterns, making them visible. Further, the women provided the male boss with just the kind of foils he needed to bring out and view his imbedded authority patterns.

Until we become aware of them, we are prisoners to our family-of-origin dynamics. But, if we feel our feelings fully, we can let these enslavements go. Unreleased family-of-origins issues are constantly repeated in the workplace. They govern the relations between people at work perhaps more than any other factor.

Healing and the Work Group

It is well known to those who have done personal growth work in groups that the group setting is a powerful context in support of individual healing. Though the workplace brings up the original family dynamics, with all its pain and wounding, it can be a wonderful place to heal the old pain. To do so, however, it must be an emotionally safe and supportive environment.

Unfortunately, few workplaces in our society have a culture that is emotionally safe and supportive. Some are, and in those healing work can be done. Most work groups, however, have cultures that emphasize competition and aggression. They are not a safe place to feel and share our pain. In fact, at work, we are usually careful not to reveal our private selves for fear others may use what they learn against us.

Therefore, most work groups are not places where we can actually process the feelings that the workplace brings up. For most of us, we have to do the feeling and release work alone, or with trustworthy others outside the workplace. In these cases, the work group serves as a stimulus for healing rather than a place to heal. It is brilliant at bringing up the material that lies clogged beneath the surface and interferes with creating and sustaining positive relations in our work lives.

To do the self-healing, we must have the courage to engage in the difficult and lonely process of going deep inside ourselves and touching the tender spot within. If there are trusted others, family, friends or fellow travelers on the path to Rekindling the Spirit, they can support us in this process. Working to release old patterns informally with others, or in a formal growth group, propels the process forward.

"Original Wounding"

When feeling our feelings becomes a daily practice we may find within us a synthesis. A central organizing block that is behind, and accounts for, many of our apparently diverse feelings. This central organizing block can be understood in terms of the concept of "original wound," an idea I learned from my partner, Barbara Lee. Original wounding refers to the time in our childhood when we abandoned our commitment to our true Self, in order to become the person our parents wanted. As children, to be supported and loved, we traded our commitment to who we truly are in order to live the image of our parents' unlived projections.

Looking within at the constricting feelings that I have experienced in my life, I have seen my central organizing block. I have a vivid image, real or symbolic, of my original wounding. It is a simple, apparently innocent, scene. I saw an image of little Howard, eight years old, sticking his head into the kitchen, at the house where I grew up. I asked my mother if I could do something I very much wanted. My mother said, "No."

Previous to that moment I would have fought to get what I really wanted. This time I simply capitulated. I was tired of the struggle to maintain my Self against this all powerful woman. I was too afraid of being the brunt of her temper again. At eight, like an old man who had fought many battles and too often lost, I quit. In that moment, I gave up the struggle to maintain full integrity.

This was the genesis of my original wound. I abandoned my Self for my mother's love and good graces. Ever since, consciously or unconsciously, I have been trying to reclaim my Self. Most of us have had similar experiences. Many of us have not, as yet, remembered.

As the popular family therapist John Bradshaw points out, maintaining a secure connection with our "source and survival relationships," our natural parents or those who acted as our parents, is the most important concern of all children. Their support for our physical survival, and their love, is central to every child. In fact, it is more dear to us than being who we truly are. As children, we are willing to abandon our Self for the support and love of our parents.

Having abandoned ourselves as children, we are not satisfied until we reclaim our identification with our true Selves as adults. We play out painful scenarios to relive the wounding of our abandonment. It continually comes to the surface to be healed.

This is the process of integrating the personality into Essence. It is moving from reactiveness into who we truly are. Releasing our original wounding is liberation from the limitations of our lineage. It is identifying and breaking the restrictions of family conditioning. We can avoid passing this wounding on to our children. They can be free to live and work in their fullness, as a result of our courage to experience and own our pain.

Sometime ago, a lawyer friend of mine was on a committee to approve the appointment of a new partner. The managing partner of the firm, who made the initial choice, recommended Ruth. My friend found himself objecting strongly to the recommendation. He argued vigorously against her and lobbied others on the committee for an alternative candidate.

Later, my friend told me, "You know, I have some insight into that situation with Ruth. Last night, before falling asleep, in that dreamy state, I saw the whole thing clearly. It was amazing. It's all connected to my family."

"Here I am, the Golden Boy in the firm, and we are adding someone new, a younger woman who I know is very capable. I was afraid Ruth might steal my glory. I would lose the attention and support I'm getting right now. I was jealous. I didn't want her, but

I didn't know why."

"Then I saw it. What it really has to do with is me and my younger sister. When I was four, my sister was born. I was pissed. First I was an only child and I had all the attention. Then, when she came along, it was like I was forgotten. The sun went out. She became the center of everything, and I was nothing special."

"Hiring Ruth brought up all those feelings. I felt cold and empty inside, but at the time I didn't know why. I got stuck in my head, arguing about why she couldn't do the job. But that really didn't have much to do with it. I was just reacting."

As he talked the situation out and got clear about its origin, it was obvious that my friend was releasing both his resistance to Ruth and the core of his own hurt. We could both feel the exhilaration of his liberation from this old limiting pattern.

The Effect of Our Parents Attitude On Our View of Work

Our parents' attitudes towards work are the foundation upon which we build our own. Our parents' views of work are the first images we have and therefore the most powerful.

Everyday, as children, we formed opinions about work by observing the behavior and listening to the words of our elders. Our parents or parent figures, the most important people in our lives, modeled to us the meaning of work. All future patterns of our relationship to work evolve from that set point.

For most of us, father was the parent who modeled the nature and meaning of work. For others it was mother, and for many, it was both. If they saw work as a joy, we are likely to feel enthusiasm for the adventure of work. If they saw work as drudgery, we are likely to find ways to avoid it. Of course, our beliefs and attitudes about work are complex and have origins in many sources, but our basic template was formed through observing the attitudes of our parental figures.

My father was a butcher, an entrepreneur who owned his own shop. For many years he was in partnership with his brothers, then he went on his own. He worked hard. He got up six days a week at

4:30 a.m. He dressed and went to the slaughterhouse to buy meat, and then on to his shop.

My dad worked a long day and came home around six in the evening, sometimes later. After work, his main interest was a meal, rest, and then sleep. I remember him as always tired. It seemed such a monumental effort for my dad to get out of bed in the morning. The vision of him, in the dark of the early morning, sitting on the edge of the bed, feet on the floor, in his underclothes trying to wake up, is a powerful lasting image.

This intense symbolic message, that work is exhausting, is deeply programmed in me, something that I have to feel and heal on a continuing basis. I have the tendency to make work hard even when it is not. When I feel this constriction, usually in my chest, I know it is time to lighten and remember who I truly am.

The bright side of what my father modeled to me about work was his masterful craftsmanship. When I went to the store and saw him at his trade, it was obvious he was very skillful and enjoyed it. He was focused and absorbed when he was working. He created the aire of the artist when he worked. I learned from my father that you can throw your whole self into work and through it find satisfaction and joy.

My mother was an idealist and romantic. From her, I inherited my love for the arts. Besides helping in my father's store, she painted and made crafts which she sold to merchants and others, directly from our home. From her I learned that work is art, that artistry is rewarded, and that like my father, one can be independent and make a living.

Two years ago I was speaking in Los Angeles and the Master of Ceremonies requested from me an exercise related to my presentation that the audience could do as a warm up. I asked them to recall their parents attitudes about work and think how it affected them. Then, to share with the person sitting next to them as much of that insight as was comfortable.

As the audience was doing the exercise, I walked around the room. I was impressed with the depth with which people were sharing. The question, even in a somewhat formal setting, evoked moving insights and deep discussions between people. One man said,

"My father was the manager of a famous night club in New York. When I was growing up, I'd walk down the street with him. I can remember it taking hours to walk the two blocks from the club to his car, because so many people knew him and wanted to talk with him." The man said that after only brief reflection on the question, it was obvious to him that since his childhood he had devoted his life to becoming famous, but all the while he did not consciously know he was trying to imitate his father. He spoke movingly about how he had sacrificed two wives and innumerable relationships in his desperate attempt to recreate the fame of his father in himself.

EXERCISE

Our Parents and our Work

- Close yours eyes and relax. Put your attention on your breath. Allow any tension to be released in your exhaling breath. Feel yourself getting fully relaxed from toes to head.
- Bring to mind your father, or someone who acted as your father, when you were a child. Bring his face into clear view.
- Look at him, without emotion, and recall what you learned about work from his model.
- Let his face recede and bring your attention back to the breath. Notice it as it goes in and out. Exhale any tension that may have been built up on the exhaling breath.
- Now bring to mind your mother, or someone who acted as your mother, when you were a child. Bring her face into clear view.
- Look at her, without emotion, and recall what you learned about work from her model.
- Synthesize what you learned about work from both your father and mother and notice how that is influencing you now.

Educational Violence

Not all of our childhood wounding occurred in the family setting. A place where it happened often, outside of the family, was school. All of us have pain that remains from those days. From bully teachers and bully schoolmates, we have experienced educational violence.

Just as the workplace simulates the family, it also simulates school. The workplace is similar in structure and process to school. It is the place we go off to in the morning and where we spend most of our day. We are enmeshed in an authority structure and have heavy expectations imposed upon us. We are judged, criticized, and rewarded.

Wounding from our school days can be reactivated at work. For instance, if our teachers abused their authority over us, we are likely to be untrustful of our bosses. If authority in our childhood was fair and consistent, we are likely to be comfortable with it at work.

For me, I have to be careful of the tendency to fall into the "pleaser" role which my educational experience rewarded. When I feel myself falling into it, in the presence of people in authority, or into its reactionary opposite, the rebel role, I know I need to stay with the feeling itself and not take the story on the outside too seriously.

The educational system, through a significant number of teachers, communicates a strong sense of limitation as to what is possible for each of us. The message is passed, "You're not good at this, you're not good at that . . . ." These limits are generally the projections of the teachers own fear and self-limitations.

One of the most common forms of educational violence is the abuse of our natural creative capacity. "You can't draw, you can't sing, you're no good at creative writing," and so on. How many of us were told we were not capable in one or all of the creative arts? Each time that limitation was imposed on me, in my childhood, I believed it, imposed it on myself, and the incapacity became real.

One of the strongest negative messages around creativity programmed into me in school was, "You can't sing." I bought it. Then a few years ago at Esalen, a friend of mine, Emmet Miller, who is very musical laughed at me when I said I couldn't sing. He said, "Can you talk? Then you can sing."

His words penetrated my defensive armor. Since that time, I sing more often, take more risk with it, use song in my work, and generally have a lot of fun with music.

We limit ourselves by believing we can't. Over the years I have overcome other blocks to expressing my natural creativity and it has been invaluable in my work. After so many years of negative programming in school about not being able to draw, I freed myself to paint. I have allowed myself to write poetry.

This process has been extremely liberating and very important to my work. Not only do I use drawing and writing directly with clients, the essential creative process that I learned through the arts guides all the work I do.

It is the way I learned to trust my intuition, take risks, allow my inner guidance to direct my actions, and to take the appropriate next step.

Conclusion

The workplace is a setting that surfaces the pain of our childhood wounds. Because it simulates the family, we can feel and heal many of the old wounds from that setting. It is also a place that brings up for attention and healing the pain we felt from educational violence.

Despite the fact that the problems we have with others at work can feel dreadful, depressing, and hopeless, they aren't. The interpersonal discomfort that the work group presents can be the ground from which we learn about ourselves and find the freedom, openness, and creativity to Rekindle the Spirit in Work.

About the Author

Howard Schechter, Ph.D., is a student of sociology, psychology, philosophy, and religion. He works as a consultant, trainer, and counselor in the areas of individual and organization development. He is former Chairman, Founder, and Professor in the Department of Organization Development and Transformation at the California Institute of Integral Studies in San Francisco, California, and creator of the Rekindling the Spirit in Work seminars.